Tiger in the Toilet

Tiger in the Toilet

Simple ways to lead a happy life

K AJAYAKUMAR

JAICO PUBLISHING HOUSE

Ahmedabad Bangalore Bhopal Bhubaneswar Chennai
Delhi Hyderabad Kolkata Lucknow Mumbai

Published by Jaico Publishing House
A-2 Jash Chambers, 7-A Sir Phirozshah Mehta Road
Fort, Mumbai - 400 001
jaicopub@jaicobooks.com
www.jaicobooks.com

TIGER IN THE TOILET
ISBN 978-81-8495-137-0

First Jaico Impression: 2010
Third Jaico Impression: 2011

Printed by

Introduction

While waiting for an indefinitely delayed flight at New Delhi airport, I was observing a gentleman sitting a few yards away from me. He was engrossed in a book. I had watched him read for more than two hours, and his face hadn't registered any emotion other than deep seriousness. Out of sheer curiosity I glanced at the book's cover. I was shocked beyond belief! He was reading *The World's Greatest Jokes*.

This gentleman represented the most unhappy and miserable human being on Earth — unable to see the goodness around him, receiving even jokes with extreme seriousness. To lead a happy life all one needs is a mind that sees goodness in and around itself. To see goodness, one's mind has to become meditative, and to make the mind meditative, one has to selflessly offer one's service to society. Any act, the primary objective of which is to benefit others, is called service. The difference between a selfish act and service is that by doing the former the doer is benefited, and others *may* also be benefited, whereas by offering our service, the benefit is felt by others and the doer as well.

The more one serves others, the more meditative and happy one becomes. The first story in this book illustrates this principle.

Tiger in the Toilet

Once a stranded tiger entered the washroom in a corporate office and hid in a dark corner. Since there were people outside the washroom through the day, the tiger was afraid to come out. Many people frequented the washroom, but the frightened tiger didn't touch anyone. However, after four days it couldn't bear hunger anymore, so it caught a man who had come in, and ate him. This man happened to be an Assistant General Manager in the organisation, but nobody noticed his disappearance. Since nothing untoward happened, The tiger became more bold and after two days caught another man and ate him. This man was the General Manager of the organisation. Still, nobody worried over his disappearance (some people were even happy that he was not seen in the office).

Next day, the tiger caught the Vice President who was a terror in the organisation. Again nothing happened. The tiger was very happy and decided that this was the perfect place for him to live.

The very next day the happy tiger caught a man who

had entered the washroom while balancing a tray of teacups in one hand. The frightened man fell unconscious. Within fifteen minutes a huge hue and cry ensued, and everyone in the office started looking for the man. The search team reached the washroom, flushed out the tiger and saved the unconscious man. He was the tea supplier in the office.

Reflection

It is not the position, but our usefulness to others that makes us lovable and respectable.

This book contains such simple and interesting stories and morals, which will entertain and educate the reader. The anecdotes in this book, arranged alphabetically according to the themes they address, will also be particularly useful for trainers, salesmen, teachers, managers and others who wish to make their presentations more effective.

ACCIDENT

1.   This seems to be a dangerous cliff," said the tourist. "It's a wonder that they haven't put up a warning sign!"

"They had one up for two years," the guide admitted, "but no one fell over, so they took it down."

Reflection

One should not wait for an accident to happen to put up a warning sign.

---

2.   A seminar on accident prevention was underway. The speaker took out 500 small tablets and spread them out on the table. Then he reached out for a small glass bottle, took out one tablet that looked similar to those on the table and kept it with the others on the table.

"There are 501 tablets on this table. The first 500 I kept on the table are ordinary painkillers. But the one I added just now, contains Potassium Cyanide. I wonder if anybody in this group would like to take a chance by consuming one tablet. Your chance of getting the Cyanide tablet is one in 501."

Reflection

Each time one takes a chance and ignores safety measures,

he/she is taking a risk. The risk could be one in million, one in thousand, one in hundred, one in ten, or just one. If it is just one, the consequences of a dangerous act will never be known. Hence, it is always better to abide by safety measures, even if one thinks that the risk is only one in million.

ACCUSING

3.   A husband and wife had the rare opportunity of meeting each other in hell. The surprised husband asked, "Why you are here? What reason did they give you for sending you here?"

"I was accused," she sadly replied, "of not showing enough kindness to fellow humans. And how about you? Why are you here?"

He thought for a moment and said, "I am here, for showing kindness to a woman who didn't show kindness to fellow beings."

Reflection

An ordinary man always accuses others for his failure. By accusing others, you are projecting yourself as an ordinary, unsuccessful person.

ADDICTION

4. A man who had consumed lots of alcohol, got into a boat and started rowing. He rowed for two hours but couldn't reach the opposite bank. After the alcohol wore off, he saw that that he had forgotten to untie the boat from the pole.

Reflection

We get addicted to unwanted beliefs, superstitions, and prejudices and try to cross the river of sorrow to reach the bank of happiness. But because of our addiction we always forget to untie the rope (attachment), which holds us back to the place where we are.

ADVERTISEMENT

5. A nine year old Sunday school youngster was the only one in his class who responded when the teacher asked if anyone knew the story of Peter. The teacher asked him to narrate the story to other students. Upon completing the narration accurately, the teacher complimented him on being the only student who had read the Bible lesson that week.

The boy, painfully honest, corrected the teacher, "I didn't read it in the Bible." He explained, "it was on a bubble gum wrapper."

Reflection

One should advertise one's message using the right medium and in the right way to get the attention of the audience.

ANGER

6.   When Alexander the Great was starting out to invade India, his wife asked him to bring her a 'Rishi' (sage) on his return, since she believed he would have great knowledge and wisdom. She wanted to learn about the soul, and life after death.

Alexander promised he would do this, and found a Rishi in India and asked him to accompany him. But the Rishi refused. It was for the first time that anyone had disobeyed Alexander. He got angry and drew his sword. On seeing the sword the Rishi smiled. This was the first time that anyone had smiled on seeing Alexander's sword. Astonished, Alexander asked, "What made you smile? Don't you know I am going to kill you?"

The Rishi replied, "Before you use your sword I want you to know two things. First, you cannot kill me with that sword. And second, you are a slave of my slaves."

Alexander demanded an explanation.

"You see, you can only cut my body with that sword but I am not of this body — I am something else. That's why I said that you cannot kill me with the sword."

"And why did you call me a slave of your slaves? You know I am the emperor of the world," Alexander shouted.

"I have conquered anger and desire to such an extent that they have become my slaves. I never obey them but rather, *they obey me*. But in your case, you succumb to anger and desire as a slave would. Am I not right then that you are a slave of my slaves?" the Rishi asked.

Reflection

Do not become a slave of a slave.

ANTICIPATION

7. A man was feared by his employees for the caustic memos he used to write. One day, one of his assistants discovered to his immense horror that he'd given the boss a set of wrong figures. Knowing well what would happen next, he fearfully started writing to the boss — 'In answer to your memo of tomorrow....'

Reflection

To carry out any duty successfully, one should anticipate the consequences of one's actions.

APPRECIATION

8.   "I am a unique actor," the actor told a film director. "I can fly." Then he took off, circled the room a couple of times and made a perfect landing.

"So you can imitate birds," the director said casually. "What else can you do?"

Reflection

Never fail to appreciate another person's efforts and capabilities.

9.   At a farewell party for an employee, all these who had gathered said many good things about him. Finally, it was the turn of the Director (Personnel) to speak. He started his speech thus, "If all of us had realised half of the good words that we have uttered today, this gentleman would not have thought about leaving our organisation..."

Do not wait for someone to resign to praise his contributions.

ARGUMENT

10. Discussions are the exchange of ideas and intelligence. Arguments are the exchange of ignorance.

People meet and exchange their ignorance when they argue. When two intelligent people meet they will not argue, but they will carefully listen and try to understand the other person's point of view.

BLAMING

11. A man, whose proposal for marriage was turned down, told the girl, "If I had all the qualities you wanted in a man, I'd have proposed to someone else!"

Reflection

When you point one finger at others, remember, three are pointing towards you.

---

12. A man said to his friend, "My family says that I am a failure. But, I now understand that it is not me, but my father who is the biggest failure in my family."

"Why is that?" the friend asked.

"Because he spent his whole life trying to make me good, but failed."

Reflection

We blame the whole world for all our problems. We should realise what we contribute towards this and correct ourselves.

---

13. During cross-examination, the defendant's lawyer asked the witness, "When you went to Mr. Henry's house the day after the incident, what did he say?"

"I object to this question," the lawyer for the prosecution interrupted.

They argued for more than an hour over this, but finally the judge allowed the question.

"Yes," started the defendant's lawyer again. "When you went to Mr. Henry's house the next day what did he say?"

"Nothing," replied the witness. "Mr. Henry was not in his house and I couldn't meet him till today."

Reflection

If everyone could utilise the time they wasted on criticising and blaming others, they could achieve a lot.

BOASTING

14. An American, an Englishman, and an Indian were talking.

"In our country the airplane touches the sky while flying," the American said.

"Will it really touch the sky," asked the others.

"Not exactly, it flies an inch below the sky," he replied.

"Our ships can sail above water," the Englishman said.

"Will it not touch the water at all?" the other two asked.

"Not exactly, the ships sink just one inch in the water," he replied.

"In our country people eat through their nose," said the Indian.

"Through the nose?" screamed the other two.

"Not exactly, just one inch below the nose," the Indian said.

Reflection

When you boast, others will notice, though they may not show it.

BORE

15. Definition of a bore — A person who tells you how to make a watch if you ask him the time.

BOSS

16. A couple of employees were discussing their new boss over a cup of tea.

"You can't help liking that guy," said one, "if you don't, he fires you."

Reflection

Your subordinates should like you not because disliking you will endanger their career, but because you are really respectable.

17. The official car of a businessman crashed into a tree and sustained heavy damages. The driver was on the verge of tears. Soon a crowd gathered there. An old man, travelling in another car, stopped, walked over to the accident site and talked to the driver compassionately, "I suppose that you will have to get the car repaired with your own money."

"Yes sir."

"Well then," said the old man. "Here is a 500-Rupee note for you. I am sure that these kind people gathered here will help you out as well."

Seeing the old man's generosity, many people contributed. Soon, the driver had collected enough money for the repairs. A bystander praised the old man whose idea it was to start the collection.

"He is a smart guy," the driver admitted, "he is my boss."

Reflection

A person who is capable of and willing to help his employees through difficult situations, is a real boss.

---

18. An angry boss screamed, "I am the boss. You are nothing. You understand? Tell me who you are?"

"I am nothing."

"And who am I?"

"The boss of nothing."

Reflection

Always try to make the subordinate something and be a boss of something, rather than nothing.

---

19. "You are next to an idiot," an angry boss shouted at the subordinate.

"Okay. I will move a little," answered the subordinate.

Reflection

If a subordinate is an idiot, the blame lies with the boss. He is not capable of moulding the subordinate into a capable person. So the boss should think twice before calling a subordinate an idiot.

---

20. The manager of a shop saw a staff member arguing with a customer.

"I saw you arguing with the customer. In this shop the customer is always right. You understand."

"Yes sir."

"Now tell me, what were you arguing about?"

"Well... he said that you are an idiot."

Reflection

Never try to gag your subordinates. It will make you look like an idiot. Encourage them to speak out. They will take care of you.

---

21. Boss: If Mr. Desai comes to see me, tell him that I'm out.

Secretary: Yes, sir.

Boss: And don't let him see you working. Or, he will not believe you.

Reflection

Lack of accountability makes policing essential. To become a responsible boss, one has to delegate responsibilities, provide freedom and make subordinates accountable for their decisions.

---

22. Brigadier Sethi and his wife were on a safari in a thick jungle. Mrs. Sethi was carrying her husband's gun in one hand and the camera in the other. Suddenly, a tiger sprang out from behind a bush, seized Brigadier Sethi and started to drag him into the bush. Mrs. Sethi lost her presence of mind and stood still, unable to move.

"Shoot!" Brigadier Sethi screamed.

"I can't. I have run out of film." Mrs. Sethi replied.

Reflection

In real life, one has to adopt appropriate methodologies to deal with situations as and when they arise. One should use a hammer to drive in a nail, a spanner for a bolt, a screwdriver for a screw, etc. Similarly, different people need to be handled differently. There are some people, who are able to judge people well and treat people correctly, they are successful managers.

23. An Army *jawan* went on a two-week holiday. After ten days, the Commander received a telegram, "No death, no emergency. But want to enjoy one more week's holiday. Request leave sanction."

The commander replied, "Happy to note your honesty. Leave sanctioned."

Reflection

The first step towards becoming a good boss is to have integrity and help the subordinate acquire that.

24. The King of Khari had two ministers, Min and Chin. Min was sincere and used to perform his duties promptly. But Chin was lazy and tried to please the King by praising him all the time. The King liked the just and sincere Min more than the flattering Chin. This made Chin jealous of Min.

One day the King went out hunting along with Chin. En route they had to walk a short distance. The road was dusty and the King's legs became dirty. Chin found the right opportunity to show his loyalty to the King. He said, "I will not allow dust to fall on your Majesty's legs." And he started cleaning the King's legs with a cloth.

On returning to the palace the King told Chin, "I am very happy with the service rendered by you while we were in the forest. You are very good at cleaning legs. Henceforth, I would like to give you the job of cleaning my legs. That will suit you more than the present job."

Reflection

One who is ready to perform his duty will try to please his boss by being prompt and accurate. But one who is not prepared to discharge his duties properly will try to get out of it by flattering his boss. Like the King of Khari, a manager should discourage flattery and encourage duty consciousness. This will raise his image among his subordinates.

CHANGE

25. A man went to a Zen master to learn about Zen philosophy. The Zen Master welcomed the man and poured tea in a cup. He kept on pouring the tea though the cup had started overflowing. The man

interrupted and asked, "Don't you see the cup is full? It cannot take any more tea!"

"That's precisely what I want to tell you," replied the master. "You are already have a lot of ideas of your own. There is no space for me to fill it with my ideas."

Reflection

One should always be open to change.

---

26. If a cow's head is pointing towards the east, in which direction is its tail pointing?

Towards the west.

No, towards the ground.

Reflection

Though change is the only permanent thing in the world, there are some facts about the universe that are always true.

COMMITMENT

27.   A successful businessman was teaching his son some business tricks.

"I attribute all my success," said the businessman, "to two things. Honesty and common sense. Honesty, my son, means keep your word at any cost."

"And," asked the young man, "what is common sense."

"Common sense," replied the senior, "is never to give it."

Reflection

Never commit to something which you are sure you won't do.

28.   During a free eye check-up camp, the doctor told a patient, "You will be able to read after this operation."

"That is very good news," the jubilant patient replied, "I never knew how to read before."

Reflection

Check all details before making any commitment.

COMMON SENSE

29. A woman tried to read the instructions on the can to open it. But she found the letters too small to read. So she went to pick up her glasses. By the time she got back, the cook had opened the can and had started cooking.

"How did you manage to open the can," asked the woman.

"When you can't read," replied the cook, "you have to think."

Reflection

The aim of literacy and higher education is to help improve common sense and thinking capabilities. It is not to be depended upon for finding solutions for all problems. Instead education should help one think and find a solution by oneself.

COMMUNICATION

30. Once a scholar wrote a six-page letter to his friend. He ended the letter with one sentence, "I could have written a much shorter letter, but I didn't have the time."

It requires a lot of preparation to make your communication
brief and concise. Without preparation one tends to beat
around the bush.

---

31. A man met his best friend from his college days,
after many years and decided to pay a visit to his house.
While leaving the house, he drew his friend's four-year-
old child close to him and said, "I am sure that by the
time we meet next you would've grown another foot."

"But I don't require another foot," protested the child.

One should take care to communicate in the receiver's
language.

---

32. A young man had a pleasant surprise when a
beautiful young woman greeted him in a party. But he
couldn't recognise her.

Then the cheerfulness vanished and he was horror-
struck when she came close to him and said, "I think
you are the father of two of my children."

The puzzled man stared at her and looked helplessly at his wife standing a couple of feet away.

What the young woman didn't realise was that there was a serious lapse in her communication. She was the teacher in the primary school where that man's two children had studied.

Reflection

A communication gap is created when one assumes that the receiver already knows things that one has in one's mind. To be an effective communicator, one should not make such assumptions, but speak clearly.

---

33.   Once a young astrologer visited the house of a rich man. He was received well and asked to predict the man's future. After a few calculations, the astrologer said, "All your relatives will die before you." On hearing this, the rich man got very angry, scolded the astrologer, and sent him away without any reward.

Later, when the young astrologer met his Guruji, he told him about the incident. The Guruji asked him to disguise himself and accompany him. Both of them went to the same rich man. The Guruji was also asked to predict the future. After some calculations he exclaimed, "What a lucky man! You will live long, longer than all your relatives."

The rich man was very happy and rewarded the Guruji.

While returning, the young astrologer asked, "You also said the same thing. But, he scolded me and rewarded you."

"It is not only the message, but how you tell it, which is also equally important," replied Guruji.

Reflection

One can make one's ideas acceptable by putting it across in the right way.

---

34. The lawyer was cross-examining a witness in an accident case.

"I think..." started the witness, but couldn't proceed further, as the lawyer interrupted and said, "We don't care what do you think. Please tell what happened."

"If you don't want to hear what I think," replied the witness, "I may as well go out of the witness box. I can't speak without thinking, I'm not a fool."

Reflection

If everyone spends some time thinking about what they should speak, then lots of troubles can be avoided.

COMPETITION

35.   A man was explaining why he had three wives, "Monopoly is always damaging. Competition improves service."

Reflection

In an organisation, the best way to improve service is to encourage competition.

CONCLUSION

36.   A youngster saw a pretty young girl standing in a crowded bus. He got up and offered his seat to her. But she declined his offer.

"You must take this seat," he said, "I insist."

"You may insist as much as you want," she replied. "I am getting down here."

Reflection

Don't jump to conclusions.

CONFIDENCE

37. A reporter, interviewing a man who was celebrating his ninety ninth birthday, said "I certainly hope I can return next year and see you reach one hundred."

"I don't see why not, young fellow," the old man replied. "You look healthy enough to me"

Reflection

Always be confident.

CULTURE

38. A quarrel erupted between a temple priest and a butcher.

"You," called out the butcher, "blood sucker, urine drinker, shit eater…"

"And you," retorted the priest, "milk drinker, fruit eater…"

Onlookers were wondering why the priest was saying all good things about a person who was shouting such bad words. One of them asked the priest why he was doing this.

"He said the names of things he eats and drinks,"

replied the priest, "and I said what I do."

A person's words and behaviour can say a lot about their culture and class.

CUSTOMER

39.   In a hotel in Delhi, a businessman asked the receptionist if the room had the facility of hot and cold water.

"Yes," said the clerk. "Hot in summer and cold in winter."

He profts, most who serves best.

40.   During an office meeting, an employee, known for overshooting the time limit, asked the Chair how long he could take to speak. Immediately came the reply, "You can take as long as you want. But the meeting will end in 15 minutes and we will all leave."

Reflection

A speech is for the audience, and not for the speaker. It should be tailor-made for the audience.

---

41. During a company meeting, everybody was offering suggestions on how to make better dog food. A trainee suggested, "Sir, I am not a dog. Let's get a few dogs here and place before them specimens of different kinds of food and see their reaction. Let us then make the one they like most."

Reflection

Ask the customer what he needs.

---

42. A village shopkeeper was playing cards with his friends at the back of his shop when a customer arrived. His friends tried to bring this to his notice.

"It's okay," he said while continuing with the game. "Just keep quiet and they will go away."

Reflection

Opportunities are like customers. If you keep quiet, they will go away. But along with them will go your prosperity and happiness and it is hard to bring them back.

CUSTOMER CARE

43. There was a dictator who provided telephones to all his generals. The specialty of the phone was that they had only earpieces and no mouthpieces.

Reflection

Provide all your customers with telephones, but remember to give them the mouthpiece also, so that they can tell you where you have to improve.

---

44. A housewife ordered 24 mangoes but received only 21 from the shop. But, the bill showed that they had charged her for 24 mangoes. She immediately called up the shopkeeper and demanded an explanation.

"Yes madam," the shopkeeper replied, "while we were transporting it, three mangoes were damaged, and since we want to improve our customer service we removed those mangoes ourselves to avoid trouble for you."

Reflection

Often we provide rotten service to our internal/external customers and yet we boast of improvements.

45. A fully computerised business establishment sent one of its customers a bill for Rs. 0.00. The customer, being extremely honest, wrote to the firm that he did not owe anything to them and requested them to stop sending such bills. However he kept on receiving reminders for an early settlement of the bill. Fed up, he sent a cheque for Rs. 0.00. A few days later he got a letter thanking him for the settlement of his dues and the receipt for Rs. 0.00 from the firm.

You should immediately clear your dues of $0.00

Reflection

While technology upgrades and computerisation are necessary to keep pace with the fast growing business environment, businesses should never lose customer orientation and the human touch.

46. In a restaurant a waiter asked, "Have you placed your order, Sir?"

"Yes," replied the man, "but I would like to make a request."

Reflection

Often customers don't even get their basic requirements fulfilled. This is true in the case of internal customers. When a customer's orders, requests, and pleas go unheeded, history shows that such organisations do not survive for long.

---

47. A man lost his sense of hearing completely and his organisation was unable to give him any job. Then one man had a brainwave, "Why don't we put him in the complaint department?"

Reflection

History shows that all organisations that turn a deaf ear to customer complaints and suggestions never last for long.

---

48. Three partners were discussing their new theatre project.

First partner: Let's charge Rs. 300 and cover all seats with leather.

Second: No, we should charge Rs. 200 and cover all seats with velvet.

Third: I think we should charge Rs. 100 and cover all seats with customers.

Reflection

The sole objective of any business is to attract and take care of customers. Failure to do this will cause the failure of the business.

DEATH

49. The servant of a rich man went to the market, and returned terrified.

"I saw Death in the market. It was staring at me. I am afraid. I would like to go back to my village, far from here and keep away from Death. Kindly give me your best horse so that I can reach my village before sunset," the servant said in a single breath.

The rich man agreed and gave him a horse. Then he himself went to the market and saw Death.

"Why did you scare my servant?" asked the rich man.

"I didn't scare him. I was surprised to see him here in this town. I was supposed to take his life this evening at his village which is quite far away from here," replied Death.

Reflection

One cannot escape death, but should accept it bravely.

---

50. Napoleon Bonaparte was a great warrior. He fought many wars and ruled most of the world. But finally a cat caught him.

Mahatma Gandhi neither fought any war, nor had he occupied any position. But he ruled many minds in India. He was also caught by the cat.

Buddha preached and converted people to good human beings. Everyone loved him. But this cat didn't spare him either.

This cat doesn't spare any one — scholars, politicians, saints, anyone. So everybody is afraid of it.

But the poor cat doesn't want to scare anybody, it moves around without making any noise and cries softly.

This cat (death) is simple, soft, and lovable. But we traditionally draw a terrifying picture about this lovely friend, and this creates fear in everybody's mind. Imagine a person suffering from old age and not being able to die. His life will be terrible. This friendly cat comes along and takes the man with it to help him rest in peace. Why can't we love such a friendly cat?

DECISION MAKING

51. A young man was searching for a girl to marry. But each girl he selected, his mother disapproved of, citing some reason or another. Fed up, he approached a friend for advice. "That's no problem. You locate a girl like your mother. She will like her." the friend suggested.

But after a few days he was more upset than before. On seeing the friend he said, "As you suggested, I looked for a girl who resembled my mother and she liked her too."

"Then what is the problem? You can marry her."

"But my father," the young man said, "hates her."

It's in your moments of decision that your destiny is shaped.

---

52. A bachelor is a person who can change his mind without needing to go home to consult anyone.

In an empowered organisation one can find a lot of bachelors, one need not always consult the boss before taking a decision.

---

53. Salesman: Those glasses make you look ten years younger, madam.

Customer: Then I don't want them. I do not want to look ten years older each time I remove them.

Everything has a positive and negative aspect. One should be able to see both and strike a balance before taking a decision.

---

54. Question: There are three frogs on a leaf. If one of them decides to jump off the leaf into the water, how many frogs are left on the leaf?

Answer: Three. Because the frog only *decided* to jump! It didn't actually jump!

Ponder over this. Are you not unlike this frog; who decides to do something, but ends up not doing anything? In life, we have to make many decisions. Some easy, some hard. Most mistakes are not made because of wrong decisions, but due to indecision. We have to live with the consequences of our decisions.

DIFFERENT POINTS OF VIEW

55. A psychiatrist began counselling a patient, asking the questions he routinely did.

"If I cut off both your ears, what will happen?" he asked.

"I will not be able to see clearly."

"Think again, I am cutting off your ears."

"Yes. If you remove both my ears I will not be able to see clearly."

"But why?"

"If you remove my ears, how will I wear my glasses?"

To be successful and happy one should be able to see at least one step ahead. But since almost every person in the world does not have this habit, they will think those who can do this are 'fools'.

DESTINY

56. A boy was born to a *tamashewali*. In his society all women were destined to become dancers, or comfort women, and the men became pimps or smugglers.

Like any other boy, his job was to massage the customers' legs. He used to do this every evening till late at night to earn his livelihood.

But he was free during the day. He joined a school and started studying well. He achieved the second rank in Grade 12. As nobody, not even his mother, knew who his father was, he didn't have a community certificate to avail of any reservation facility. He got admission in the medical college in the general merit category and also received a scholarship. He became a doctor, married a doctor, and they opened a clinic for the downtrodden.

A boy destined to become a pimp, became a social reformer and guiding force for his own society because he decided to change his destiny by sheer labour.

Not only that one boy, but all human beings have the
capacity to change their destiny.

DEVELOPMENT

57.   A man travelled in a supersonic jet and reached
his destination two and half hours earlier than he would
have if he had travelled in a normal aircraft. Later, he
was explaining the benefit of such aircrafts to one of his
friends, "You see, it gives you an extra two and half
hours to look for your baggage."

Progress allows people extra time to do something new, not
to waste time on the same old things.

DISHONESTY

58.   A man went to a city to look for a job. He met
a shopowner and said, "I have come here to make an

honest living."

"Well," said the shopowner. "In that case you are lucky. That's the only area that doesn't have any competition in this town."

Reflection

Most problems in this world are due to dishonesty.

---

59. A rich businessman wanted to influence a minister so that he could ask for a favour. He offered the politician an imported automobile.

"I cannot accept your present," protested the politician. "I do not approve of corruption."

"Then I will not give this to you free of cost," suggested the businessman, "but I will sell you this car to you for Rs. 1000."

"In that case I would like to buy two of them," the enthusiastic politician replied.

Reflection

Just by twisting words, one wrong will not become a right.

EDUCATION

60. A Grade Six student came home from school and asked his mother if she had sex education in her school. She said that she had not had any sex education.

"Then there is no way I can ask you my doubt. You won't be able to explain," said the disappointed child.

Reflection

Formal education is not the only way of learning things. It is not correct to think that one who has received formal education knows everything, or one who has not received education knows nothing.

EFFORT

61. A man insured his house against fire. After signing the documents he asked the insurance agent, "What will I get if this building is destroyed in a fire tonight?"

"About five years," replied the agent.

Reflection

Put your thoughts in the right directions otherwise the results could be disastrous.

---

62. A small boy stood at a post office counter and said, "My friend said that if I paste a five rupee stamp on this letter it will go to Delhi."

The postal clerk replied, "Yes, it will."

The boy laughed, "That is so funny. I have written a Mumbai address on the envelope."

Reflection

To achieve anything, one has to plan correctly and put in the right efforts.

EGO

63. A teacher gave the following sentence to the students as practice for punctuation — *Woman without her man is not complete.*

Boys and girls in the class punctuated it differently.

Boys: Woman, without her man, is not complete.

Girls: Woman! Without her, man is not complete.

Reflection

Often people assume too much and think that without them the world would not survive. In the bargain they are not able to see the worth of others.

---

64. A rich woman was unhappy with her life. She went to a psychiatrist and asked for help.

"Madam," said the doctor after some prolonged consultation, "I cannot help you. But you can help yourself. My advice to you is to visit the Gateway of India and take a good, long look at something bigger than yourself."

Reflection

Nobody is 'big' in this world. If somebody feels and acts big, then he is bringing unhappiness to himself, because he will not be able to enjoy the small things that make life enjoyable.

---

65. A football player from a local club went to see a movie with his wife. As he entered the cinema hall the few people inside turned towards them and clapped. The football player was surprised to see how popular he had become among the locals.

While sitting down he leaned over to a man sitting in the front row and said, "I am surprised to see that all of you recognised me and honoured me with a standing ovation."

"I don't know you, Sir," the man shrugged. "The theatre owner had told us that he would start screening the film only after a minimum of 20 people were present in the hall. With you two we are 20 in the hall now."

Reflection

Often we assume too much about our own worth, without paying attention to the situation we are in. This happens quite often with fashion-conscious people. They wear odd dresses and assume that they have become more attractive and people are looking at them with envy. But, the truth may be that people are looking at them with sympathy.

66. A widow happened to talk to the soul of her husband.

"Are you happy there?" she asked.

"Yes, very much. I enjoy this place," he replied.

"Of course, heaven is an enjoyable place," the excited wife commented.

"Oh, no! I am in hell," came the reply.

Reflection

Due to ego and selfishness, sometimes we make someone else's life so miserable that they feel more comfortable in hell than with us.

---

67.   "My uncle and aunt didn't have even an argument for years."

"That's wonderful."

"Not exactly. Aunt stays in her native place in India and uncle is in Uganda."

Reflection

Often we are too egoistic and intolerant making it impossible to get along with others. But the 'hater' is more miserable than the 'hated'. Hence, in one's own interest it is better to get over one's ego and intolerance.

---

68.   A young man approached a bank for a loan for starting a business. The banker refused the request saying that the man did not possess enough experience. The young man tried to convince the banker. Finally the banker said, "One of my eyes is artificial. I will sanction your loan if you can identify which eye is artificial."

The young man looked into both eyes of the banker and said, "The left eye is artificial."

"How did you know that?"

"Only that eye showed a little bit of sympathy."

Reflection

Due to our inability to empathise, we make another's life miserable. Many times, our decisions are influenced by our ego rather than what the situation (or organisation) requires. One should understand that this will make us seem less respectable, though people may not be able to point this out to us.

69.   "Madam, I came to tune your piano."

"But I didn't want it to be tuned."

"You didn't madam. But your neighbours did."

Reflection

Keep an eye on your behaviour, if others seem to be taking extraordinary efforts while dealing with you. You may be guilty of being too egoistic, and they probably don't want to hurt you.

70. A lawyer addressed the judge as 'gentleman' instead of 'Your Honour'. At the end of the argument, the perfectionist judge drew the lawyer's attention towards the mistake. Immediately the lawyer rose and apologised, "In the middle of the argument, I called Your Honour a 'gentleman'. Now I realise that it was a mistake, Your Honour."

Reflection

One who insists on formalities, honorifics etc. makes a fool of himself in front of others.

---

71. One day, while leaving his chamber, a judge slipped and fell down several steps. An alarmed personal assistant rushed to him and while helping him get up asked, "I hope Your Honour is not hurt."

"No, no," replied the judge, rubbing his back. "My honour is intact but it is my back that is hurt."

Reflection

Honour is not a concrete object. It is abstract, a feeling created by your own ego. If you are wise, you will understand that this feeling will not be hurt by others not 'honouring' you and you must stop expecting such behaviour if you want to lead a blissful life.

EXPERIMENTATION

72.   "I have been in this business for 37 years," said the businessman. "Once I earned a crore one year, the next year I went bankrupt. I made up for the losses and built this business empire. I displeased many people, but I also helped many. Some people loved me, while some wanted to kill me. Many of the products I introduced, fared well in the market, while some failed."

"Now," said his friend, "since you have seen everything in this business, why don't you leave it to your children and retire?"

"No," said the businessman hurriedly, "now I am staying to see what the hell happens next."

Reflection

The best way to enjoy life is to experiment. If one is prepared to try new things, without retiring, one will always emerge victorious. And the important factor is participation, not the result. If one learns to enjoy life's experiences, one will lead a happy life.

EXPERT

73. An expert is one who knows more and more about less and less, until he knows absolutely everything about nothing.

74. "My goodness," exclaimed the man. "You charge Rs. 500 for pulling out a tooth. It is a minute's job."

"If you wish," replied the dentist, "I will pull it out slowly."

Reflection

An expert's remuneration is not determined by the amount of time he spends on the job, but the effect he has.

---

75. At the end of a lecture on goldfish, given by an expert, a member of the audience asked, "How can we identify the sex of a goldfish?"

"It is very easy," replied the goldfish expert. "You feed them a few worms and observe. The male goldfish takes only male worms and the female goldfish takes only the female worms."

"But how can one know which is the male worm and which is female?"

"That I can't say. I am only a goldfish expert, not a worm expert."

Reflection

One will be acknowledged as an expert if, and only if, he/she can offer solutions to a problem. If not, whatever knowledge he/she has acquired will be wasted.

EXPLOITATION

76. A man made a down payment of ten lakh rupees for a new luxury car. On the way home, he decided to buy some flowers. The poor flower seller was demanding Rs. 80 for a beautiful garland.

"It is very costly," the rich man said, "I can pay you only Rs. 50."

Reflection

The root of all suffering in this world is that the rich insist on exploiting the common man.

77. A bag was lost during an auction. The owner made an announcement, "A bag containing some

important documents and Rs. 10,000 is missing. Whoever returns the bag will be rewarded Rs. 500."

After a moment's silence, a voice called out, "700 rupees," placing a higher bid.

Reflection

One of the main causes of trouble in this world is the desire of people to acquire another's property.

---

78.   "How many times should I tell you to keep away from the biscuit tin?" a mother shouted at her little boy.

"Not any more, Mom, it's empty," replied the boy.

Reflection

There will be an end to all kinds of exploitation. One cannot live by exploiting people around them, one has to live a constructive life as well.

---

79.   A mother said to her little child, "Yesterday there were two chocolates in the tin. But today there is only one. Why?"

"It was dark and I didn't see the other one."

The world is too small a place for five billion people to exploit each other constantly. If we live like this child, leaving things unexploited only because we are not able to do a thorough job, we will not have many more years left to continue such a life. Hence, the conservation of resources should be given prime importance.

FASHION

80.   A fashion-conscious old lady went to a beauty parlour, had a facial and a hair cut. She doesn't look like an old lady any more, she looks like an old man.

Most of the time, fashion does not follow any logic, and fashion conscious people seem to be like buffoons. The unfortunate thing is that they do not understand this themselves.

81. An old gentleman saw a child playing in the park, but could not make out if it was a boy or a girl. So he asked the person sitting next to him on the bench, "See that child wearing jeans and a T shirt? Is that a boy or a girl?"

"It is a girl," came the angry answer. "She is my daughter."

"I am so sorry," regretted the old man, "I didn't think that you were her father."

"What?" screamed the parent, "I'm her mother!"

Reflection

One should dress to project one's personality, not to hide it.

FLATTERY

82. A newly married couple received many valuable presents when they settled down in a new apartment. Among the presents was an envelope containing two tickets for a popular show, and a small note — *Guess who sent this!*

They tried to identify the sender but couldn't. However they went for the show and had a great time. On their way back home late at night, they were wondering who had given them such a nice present. On reaching home they were shocked to see that all their valuables were missing. There was a note on the table — *Now you know who sent you the tickets!*

Reflection

Beware of people who always praise you, without giving you even a hint of your mistakes. Such people may have an ulterior motive.

FREEDOM

83. A man approached a famous sage and asked, "How much freedom have I got on this Earth, and how much I am tied to this world?"

"Please stand on one leg," asked the great sage.

The man did that. Then the sage asked him to raise the other leg. The man said that he was unable to do so.

"You are free to the extent that you can stand on one leg and you are tied to the world to the extent that you have to keep one leg on the ground," explained the sage.

Reflection

Nobody is totally free. One should gain knowledge and

maturity to understand the amount of freedom we have and live accordingly.

FRIEND

84.   Your friend is a person who knows everything about you and still likes you.

85.   A middle-aged woman asked a man to guess her age.

"I think," replied the wise man, "the trouble is whether to place you in the twenties on account of your looks, or in your forties on account of your intelligence."

Reflection

Friendly talk is the key for a friendly life.

GOAL

86.   The owner of a general store was dying. His family stood around his bed, weeping. His wife bent over the bed and sobbed, "Can you hear me? We are all here."

The dying man whispered, "Is Ravi there?"

"Yes," said the wife.

"And Ranjit?"

"Yes."

"And Rajeev?"

"Yes."

"And Rakesh?"

"Yes," his wife said.

The old man raised his head and cried out, "Then who the hell is taking care of the shop?"

Reflection

One should have a firm objective in life and always remember it, even on the deathbed.

GOOD LIFE

87. "I have heard a lot about you," a new manager told his subordinate.

"Maybe," replied the subordinate. "But you cannot prove it."

Reflection

If you do not lead a good life you cannot enjoy anything in life, not even praise.

88. An executive was telling his wife about the unusual pain he was feeling. But neither he, nor she, could understand the cause of pain. After a few days on returning from the office he told her, "I now know why I've been feeling so miserable. We had purchased some ultra modern office furniture two weeks ago and only today I learnt that I've been sitting in the dustbin."

Reflection

In the ultra-modern society many people are leading a miserable life, which they are not able to change owing to ego-centrism. If one wants to lead a happy and comfortable life, one should realise one's requirements and live accordingly, instead of blindly following others.

89. During the 90th birthday celebrations of a rich woman who was hot tempered and adamant, one of the invitees asked the lady's close relative, "Why do you think God has given her such a long life?"

"To test the patience of her relatives," came the reply.

Reflection

While nearing the end of a long life, if the person's family or friends feel that he/she was of no use to them, then the entire life seems to be a waste and there is no time to correct things. A successful person is one who realises one's purpose at a young age and lives accordingly.

90. A priest and a taxi driver died and reached the Gates of Heaven at the same time. The taxi driver was admitted first. The priest felt a little unhappy and when he got the opportunity to meet the God he started complaining, "I have been praying throughout my life. Still a taxi driver was given first preference here. Why did this happen?"

"While you preached, people slept, but when the taxi driver drove, everybody sat up and prayed," God replied.

Reflection

One's merit is judged not only by the good life one has led, but also based on how one has been able to help others lead a good life.

91. A friend asked Ravi, "Have you lived all your life here?"

Ravi said, "Not yet."

Reflection

People take birth, grow up, become old and die, but very few actually live their life. Others simply exist like any other animal. An intelligent person should understand the difference between living and simply existing. Experiment and find better ways of living each moment.

---

92.   There was a petty thief living in a village. A much feared dacoit wanted his help for a robbery. So he approached the thief and instructed him to pretend to be a sage and get the respect of the villagers so that nobody suspected him.

The thief pretended to be a sage for some time. He behaved well, learnt good things, taught village children, and extended help to everyone. In a few days, he earned the respect of everyone in the village.

After some time, the dacoit met the thief and said, "The time has come. People in the village have started respecting you, thinking that you are a good man. Now you can start robbing their houses and nobody will suspect you."

The thief thought for a moment and replied, "I have been pretending to be good for some time and people have started respecting me. After seeing the faith and respect they have for me I am not able to harm them. I love this life and I don't want to become a thief again."

Anyone who has experienced the joy of leading a good life will never prefer a bad life. A good life is like a fruit tree, and a bad life is like a weed. Generally it is difficult to plant and take care of a fruit tree, and very easy to bring up a weed. But the weed never gives you any fruits.

---

93. A small boy said, "Dad, when I grow old, will I be able to do what I wish for?"

Dad said, "Nobody lives that long, my son."

At no point of time will one be able to do whatever one wants to do. There will always be some success and some failure. One should not lose heart when something fails, or get over-excited when we achieve success either.

---

94. It was a boy's first meeting with his girlfriend's father.

"So," asked the old man. "You want to be my son-in-law, do you?"

"Eh, not exactly," replied the young man. "But, if I want

to marry your daughter I don't have much choice, do I?"

Reflection

If people come to you just because they have no other choice, then, as an individual, you are a failure. One should behave in such a way that in spite of other choices, people come to you.

---

95. A girl, who was in love with a lawyer, was terribly upset.

"What is wrong?" asked her friend. "You were always happy with your lover."

"Yes, I was," replied the girl. "But the other day he sent me a bill for services rendered for the time spent with me."

Reflection

One has to be a thorough professional at the workplace and a thorough family person at home. One will be a failure, if he/she carries work-related matters home, or feelings to the office.

---

96. A woman rushed into an aquarium and asked, "Can you get me a live shark?"

"But," replied the amazed aquarium keeper, "we don't sell sharks. Why do you want a shark after all?"

"It is for my home aquarium," replied the woman. "My neighbour's cat has been catching my goldfish. I want to teach her a lesson."

Reflection

Many people invite greater troubles just to take revenge on someone, thus making their own life miserable. A little bit of forgiveness leads to a lot of peace in everybody's life. Always it is the one who hates who is more miserable than the person hated.

97. A small business concern bought a typewriter and found a defect in it. On pressing the key 'e' it typed 's'. The steno immediately wrote a complaint to the supplier which reads as follows:

To
Ths Impsrial Company
Middls town

Dsar Sirs,

Ws ars in rscsipt of ths typswritsr ssnt by you through 'Spssd Carrisrs.'

Upon using ths typswritsr ws found silly but rathsr ssrious flaws with ths machins. Whsnsvsr ws prsss ths ksy 's', ths fifth lsttsr of ths alphabst, it typss as 's'. Thsrsfors ws rsqusst you to sithsr ssnd anothsr machins as frss rsplacsmsnt, or ssnd your mschanic for corrscting this machins, as sarly as possibls.

Yours truly,

Willss. S. Sdward
Chairman,
Canopy Publishing Company

NB: Ths nams of ths chairman is 'Wil+(two timss ths fifth lsttsr of ths alphabst)'. Ons tims ths fifth lsttsr of ths alphabst. 'Fifth lsttsr of ths alphabst+dward'"

Reflection

Life is like a typewriter and basic human values are like the letters. Even if you miss just one of them, you will end up in great trouble.

---

98. A young man was explaining why he had no interest in his job.

"There is no future in that job. The owner's daughter got married last week."

Reflection

While long-term goals are required for sustaining interest in any job, one should learn to enjoy the job itself. Otherwise one cannot enjoy any job and always feel miserable.

---

99. I have a watch which does an hour in 55 minutes.

Reflection

There is no shortcut to a good life. One has to put in hard work, and stay on the right path, to make life enjoyable. If one hurries through shortcuts, ultimately it would make life useless, as is a watch that does an hour in 55 minutes.

---

100. "Aren't you ashamed," asked the judge, "to be seen in this court so frequently?"

"No Your Honour," replied the convict. "I thought it was a respectable place."

Reflection

One can be a saint in a fish market, and one can be thief in a temple. It is not the place, but the actions that are important.

---

101. Father: You should realise which side of the bread is buttered.

Son: How does it matter? I am going to eat both sides.

Reflection

If one is prepared to face happiness and hardships and accept them as part of life, nothing else matters and he/she shall lead a happy life.

102. A woman was criticised for not having the Bible in her house.

"But I have a Dictionary in my house," she responded. "There is no word in the Bible which is not in my Dictionary."

Reflection

Just like one needs the words in the right order to make a Bible, by putting things in order one can make one's life successful and enjoyable. Religion should be practised to learn how to put things in order.

103. Once two friends decided to tell their

misdeeds to each other.

Then they didn't speak to each other for 10 years.

Reflection

One should lead such a life that even if one has to share all of one's misdeeds, one should be able to talk to others.

---

104. Ravi: My grandfather lived up to the age of sixty, but never used glasses.

Ranjit: Yes, I also have come across many people who prefer to drink directly from the bottle.

Reflection

One's perception stems from one's thinking. If you feel that everything is wrong with the world, you only have to look into yourself to find something wrong.

---

105. Mike: Johnny, you should live up to your status in the society and wear better dresses. Don't allow yourself to look so shabby.

Johnny: But I am not shabby!

Mike: You are. Recollect your father. How well he used to dress! He always looked elegant.

Johnny: That's exactly what I said. I'm wearing his dress only.

Reflection

One cannot upgrade oneself just by following others blindly. One has to apply one's mind to find out ways and means for better living.

---

106. "When I read your latest poem I started wondering—" said the critic to a poet,

"On what I was writing!" interrupted the poet.

"No," said the critic, "why did you write it?"

Reflection

Life is like a poem. What you are living for and how you are living are two equally important questions to be answered.

---

107. During an exhibition of modern art a villager asked another, "Why did they hang this picture here?"

"Because they couldn't locate the artist."

Reflection

Life is as much an art, as a science. You should lead such a life that others should always enjoy your presence, without thinking of hanging you.

---

108. Said a teenager, "I am starting to wonder what my parents were up to at my age that makes them so suspicious of me all the time!"

Reflection

One should be straightforward, so that one is trusted. If you suspect everybody, it is a proof that you are doing something wrong.

---

109. Once Hitler went to an astrologer to know the date of his death. The astrologer made some calculations and said that he would die on a Jewish holiday.

"Which Jewish holiday?" demanded Hitler.

"How does it matter?" replied the astrologer, "any day you die will be a Jewish holiday."

Reflection

One should lead such a life that people should be happy that one is alive, not that one is dead.

---

110. A rich man said, "I gave one hundred rupees to that man for saving my life."

"What did he say," asked his friend.

"Nothing. But he gave back Rs. 95," told the rich man.

Reflection

The value of your life is based on how others evaluate it, not how you evaluate it. Therefore, your deeds should be such that the value of your life increases.

GREATNESS

111. A great sculptor once was asked by his admirer, "Which is your greatest creation?"

Without hesitation he said, "My next one."

Reflection

Nothing is perfect, but to understand this, one requires a great mind.

---

112. Mark Twain, once said, "They say George Washington was great because he could not tell a lie. But I am greater than him because I can tell a lie, but I don't."

Reflection

Great people are those who don't do a bad thing, though they can, and do a good thing though they can't.

---

113. An assistant walked into the lab at 2 a.m. and found Edison smiling. Naturally the assistant assumed that Edison had surmounted a problem.

"You have solved a problem!" he said.

"Not exactly," replied the great man. "I just found out that all my assumptions about a particular problem are wrong. Now I can discard all of them and start afresh."

Reflection

The capacity to accept failure and the mental strength to start afresh, distinguishes a great man from an ordinary man.

---

114. During a marriage ceremony, one of the relatives felt that he was not given adequate importance in the seating arrangement. Later he told the bride's father, "I think you are not able to keep people in their place."

"Those who matter don't mind, and those who mind don't matter," replied the father.

Reflection

A person's greatness can be judged by his behaviour. Those who feel agitated by small issues such as seating arrangements, the way they are addressed, etc show their immaturity. And then there are great minds who do not mind such small things.

---

115. Once a man went to Fr. Vincent Perera (who was made a saint later) and said, "I'm collecting old clothes for an orphanage. Do you have any old clothes?"

"Yes, I have two old clothes with me."

"Would you donate them to me?"

"No. I cannot give them to you."

"I can assure you that they will be put to worthy use. After all, what do you do with them?"

"Every day I wash and dry one of them to wear the next day."

Reflection

Simplicity is a common quality among all great people. They are all too busy performing service to humanity to care for their appearance.

GREEDINESS

116. Jerry lost all his money in a casino, by playing cards. Heartbroken he climbed up a tree and started putting a noose around his neck. When he was about to tighten the noose, he heard a voice saying, "Don't jump, Jerry. Go back to the casino. This time I will help you. I

will tell you when and how much to bet."

Although he was not completely convinced, Jerry decided to listen to the voice. He went back to the casino. With the ring on the finger, which was the only thing he had left, he started playing. In the second round he heard the voice, "Jerry bet your ring this time." Jerry bet the ring and won. After two rounds the voice again asked him to bet all his winnings. This time too, he won. The voice helped him a few more times and Jerry won more than a million dollars. Jerry had become very happy and bold. He decided to bet all the money he had won. The voice warned him not to bet anything. But, he was in no mood to listen to any more advice. He lost. There was nothing left to bet. Disappointed Jerry went back to the tree where he had heard the voice the first time and asked the voice what to do.

"Now you can hang yourself," came the reply.

Reflection

When a man becomes greedy, he loses his sense of judgment and always stands to lose.

---

117. "I am very sad," a man told his friend.

"What's wrong?" the friend asked.

"Last month my elder uncle died and left two lakh rupees for me."

"That's bad. Still there is something to be cheerful about," the friend consoled him.

If only I had a few more Uncles...

"This month my younger uncle died and left five lakh rupees for me."

"But that is also not an absolutely bad thing," his friend wondered.

"But I am very sad," he mourned, "I just had two uncles."

Reflection

A greedy person may become wealthy, but not happy.

HABITS

118. A Professor was addressing his English Composition class students. He was reading out a particularly inept essay and as usual asked them for their comments. The students criticised it unmercifully.

"Interesting," commented the professor, "because I wrote it myself. You are quite right. It is incredibly bad. I spent two hours of painstaking effort to ensure that I had not omitted a single feature of bad writing and believe I have succeeded."

"What astounds me," he resumed, "is how you guys can make these sorts of things day after day in ten minutes."

Reflection

If you make it a habit to do good things, it will be difficult to do bad things, and vice versa.

---

119. He ran after girls when he was young. Now he has changed. He runs after women.

Reflection

Habits, good or bad, are difficult to change. So it is important to cultivate good habits.

---

120. The jail warden offered a cigarette to a man who was to be hanged the next morning.

"No! Thanks. I gave up smoking because it's bad for my health," he replied.

He wants to complete his exercise before being hanged.

There is no specific time to give up a bad habit. However, it is better not to wait for the last moment to do so.

HAPPINESS

121. A butcher, a farmer, and a rich man lived in a village. The rich man was really wealthy and he enjoyed all sorts of pleasures. But over a period of time he felt bored as if something was missing in his life.

The farmer had hundreds of acres of land and his crops were very good. But he never used to give even a handful of grains to the birds. He even had people to chase away the birds that picked grains. In spite of prosperity, he was miserable. He felt something was missing in his life.

The butcher was very cruel to the animals. In spite of a roaring business he also felt something was missing in his life.

One day a great sage came to the village. The rich man, the farmer and the butcher went to him to find out the secret to happiness. It so happened that all of them reached the sage at the same time and told him about their misery and sought his advice.

In reply the sage said only one word — 'Da'

They didn't understand what he meant. But the sage didn't utter a word after that. So they left. But they were always thinking about the meaning of 'Da'.

It was the rich man who cracked the nut first. One day he felt that the sage meant 'Damanam' (self-control). He was leading a life without any control. From that day onwards he started exercising self-control and that made him happy.

One day the farmer was chasing away the birds from his farm when suddenly he thought that probably the sage meant 'Danam' (charity) when he had uttered 'Da'. He began donating a portion of his grain, and started feeling happiness.

While he was working, the butcher noticed that an animal, who was about to be slaughtered, was crying. A thought flashed through the butcher's mind, and he felt that the sage had meant 'Daya' (mercy) by uttering 'Da'. So he started showing mercy to animals and felt happy.

Reflection

Damanam, Danam, and Daya — self control, charity, and mercy are three shortcuts to happiness and peace.

122.   There was a couple who always felt that they

would be happier in a more expensive apartment. One day their wish was fulfilled — the apartment owner raised the rent.

Reflection

Money is not a criterion for happiness.

---

123. A recent survey reveals that half the people in the world are unhappy because they can't have some of the things that make the other half unhappy.

Reflection

The root cause of happiness and unhappiness is in the mind, not in material things.

---

124. A bride kept looking out of the window through the entire first night because her mother had told her that her first night would be the most beautiful night ever, and she didn't want to miss even a single moment.

Reflection

The problem with today's world is that people do not know

what to enjoy. Everybody is trying to enjoy something, which cannot give them any happiness, and thus they leave behind some great enjoyable things, or opportunities.

125. A man went to a casino and placed a 100-rupee note on the poker table. He won the bet. Then he doubled it and won again. Every succeeding bet he won, and in just over two hours he earned more than one lakh rupees.

Now he became very confident and started making big bets. Unfortunately, in a short while he lost all that he had gained. While coming out of the casino a friend asked how he had fared.

"I lost one hundred rupees," came the cool reply.

Reflection

If people understand that the things they have in this world do not belong to them, then they can be happy. Because then, even the losses seem small.

126. "You didn't get any story during the high society wedding?" screamed the editor to the reporter who came in without a story after attending a wedding attended by all the celebrities of the city.

"Nothing sir," shrugged the reporter, "the groom didn't show up. So there was no wedding."

Reflection

To be happy, one has to be an efficient reporter. One should always report to one's mind that one is happy, no matter what the circumstances. If he/she fails to report this, then the mind does not get any news and it feels miserable. Unfortunately, most people in this world are not able to see any news (happiness) in their life's events, even though these events may be small and yet significant and pleasant.

For every 10 minutes you are angry, you lose 600 seconds of happiness.

127. A boy wanted to impress his girlfriend. So he said, "My uncle is a millionaire."

LOVE FOR A MILLION

This had a lightning effect. The girl is now ready for marriage, not with him... but with his uncle.

Reflection

Those who change their mind on seeing money may get a lot of money, but not happiness.

---

128. "He drinks a lot because he is worried too much."

"What is he worried about?"

"He is worried that he is drinking too much."

Reflection

Looking for happiness via materialism is a vicious circle. One feels that by acquiring things one can be happy, but then he/she realises that the happiness they expected is not forthcoming, and then they feel unhappy.

---

129. On seeing the pyramid a visitor said, "What a waste! So much masonry, and no rent."

Reflection

If one starts evaluating everything in terms of its monetary value, then one will not enjoy the beauty of this world. Living without enjoying the beauty of this world is a waste.

---

130. "Be careful, you will hurt your finger while you are hitting the nail with the hammer," Father cautioned little Rani.

"Don't worry Dad, I am safe. Younger brother is holding the nail for me," replied Rani.

Reflection

One may feel that one can enjoy life by passing on all hardships to others. But taking up a little bit of suffering, or hardship for others makes life more enjoyable. For a human being, sacrifice gives ultimate pleasure.

---

131. "How far can a cat chase a mouse into a bush?"

"It depends on the size of the bush."

"No. A cat can chase the mouse only halfway through. After that it is chasing the mouse out of the bush."

Reflection

Problems do not exist forever. No matter what problem one is facing, there will come a time when one is getting out of a problem. But to experience happiness, one should stop worrying about the problem and try to emerge out of it.

---

132. A middle-aged man approached the postmaster and said, "I have been getting threatening letters very frequently through your mail service. Isn't there any law to stop this? Can you do anything about this?"

"Yes, of course," replied the postmaster. "This is against the law and you can file a lawsuit against the sender. By the way, do you have any idea who's sending it?"

"Yes," said the man. "It is the company I am paying instalments to."

Reflection

Happiness and misery are created by your own actions. There is no reason why you should blame others for your misery.

---

133. "What did you learn in school today?" a mother asked her child.

"Buffoonery, mockery, jeering, quarrelling, scuffling," replied the child.

If you want to make your life happy and enjoyable, you should learn to see the goodness in everything. If you see misery, you will tend to find only negatives in everything.

134. A man bought a house in the suburbs and started planting a garden. When the plants sprouted, he wasn't able to distinguish between the plants and weeds. So he asked a neighbour.

"If you want to know the difference between plants and weeds," the neighbour replied, "just pull them out. If they grow back again they're weeds!"

Many bad habits are like weeds, difficult to destroy. But remember, they don't give fruits either.

135. There was a very happy couple. Occasionally, they quarrelled. The wife would throw utensils at the husband. If they struck him, she was happy, if they did not, he was happy. However, *they* were happy, always.

Reflection

One should learn how to create long-lasting happiness.

HEALTH

136. A doctor met a former patient during a party.

"How do you feel now?" he asked the patient.

"I'm alright now," replied the patient. "I strictly followed the instruction given on the medicine bottle given by you and it cured me."

"What was the instruction?" asked the amazed doctor.

"It said the bottle should be kept tightly corked."

Reflection

If all human beings stopped depending only on medicines for

a healthy life and started leading a natural life, many health problems could be solved.

---

137. "I'm not able to sleep" complained an insomniac to his doctor. "The least sound disturbs me. Even a cat wailing outside my bedroom keeps me awake through the night."

"This tablet," replied the doctor handing over a few small tablets, "should solve your problem."

"When should I take this?" asked the patient.

"You don't take this," said the doctor. "Dissolve it in milk and give it to the cat."

Reflection

The time has come for the human race to look at diseases from a different perspective. Instead of consuming a lot of poisonous medicines, one should start eliminating the cause of diseases by adopting a proper lifestyle.

HEAVEN

138.   A villager died and was admitted to heaven. He was shown around heaven and was asked for his opinion.

"Not bad," he said. "But personally, I prefer my village."

Reflection

If you learn to love your surroundings, you are already in heaven.

HELP

139.   In a crowded bus, a man saw his friend sitting with his eyes closed.

"What happened?" he asked.

"One thing I can't tolerate is seeing old people suffer. You see, an old man is standing there with great difficulty. I can't stand that sight," said the friend.

Reflection

If, instead of closing our eyes to the needy and suffering, we help them, the world would be a much better place to live in.

---

140. An aunt told a little girl, "Well child, I am going tomorrow. Are you sorry?"

"Yes, aunt," replied the little girl. "I thought you were going today."

Reflection

Be friendly and helpful, then you will gain the love and respect of everyone.

---

141. A sage named Atmamitra had several disciples in his ashram. One of them, Sankhan, was very naughty and used to fight with his mates. But the sage never punished him. One day Sankhan beat up a classmate. All the children complained to the sage and said, "We are unable to bear the atrocities of Sankhan. We have complained to you many times, but you never take any action. It appears that you like him more than us. You should either send him away, or we will be forced to leave the ashram."

The sage looked at the disciples and said, "You are my best students. You have gained the maturity to know right and wrong, but he has not. So he requires my help more than you. I want him to stay with me until he gains the maturity you have gained."

There is a universal tendency to help bright students while very little attention is given to slow learners. What should actually be done, is the complete opposite. Slow learners require more help.

---

142. "Why does that man have so little time for himself?"

"He must be terribly busy."

"No, it's because he gives too much time to others."

At the end of your life, a balance sheet of happiness and sorrow is presented. All the time you spent for others would appear in the happiness column and all the time spent on yourself would fall in the other column. Success is achieved only if there is a surplus in the happiness column.

HONESTY

143. Employer to the new cashier, "Honesty is very

important. When you are at the cash counter, let's say a customer gives you a 500 rupee note instead of 100, by mistake. What will you do?"

Cashier replies, "I think I have to decide whether to share it with you, or not."

Reflection

Almost all of today's problems are created because of dishonesty. An honest person is these days redefined as one who shares his dishonest earnings. The world has almost forgotten how to be honest.

---

144. "So you are looking for a job, eh?" asked the proprietor. "Do you like hard work?"

"No, Sir,"

"I'll take you for this job. This is the only honest answer I've got from a candidate till today"

Reflection

Honesty pays, sooner or later.

---

145. A lean man, who looked very weak and pale, applied for a job that required heavy physical effort.

While interviewing him the manager showed him the other well-built and tough workmen engaged in the job and asked him if he would be able to work like those macho men.

"Well," replied the candidate looking at those tough guys. "I may not be able to do as much as those guys can, but I definitely will be able to do as much as they are doing."

Reflection

The primary consideration during the selection of an employee should be his sincerity and ability to work hard. A hardworking employee with fewer talents contributes more than a talented, but lazy, one.

HUMAN VALUES

146. Two villagers met in the city. They hadn't seen each other for many years.

"How long you have been staying here?" asked the first one.

"Long enough to feel at home," replied the second villager.

"How is that?" asked the first.

"I can occupy a seat in a bus even as an old man stands and not even think about him," replied the second.

A change cannot be called 'development' if it does not promote human values. That's the reason why urbanisation has created more troubles for people than it has solved.

---

147. One villager had settled down in a town. One day, he was narrating his experience to a friend.

"The first thing I did," he said, "on reaching the town, was to open a bank account. But that bank was not good."

"What happened?" asked the friend.

"Only a week later they returned my cheque for Rs. 1000, saying there were 'No Funds'," complained the villager.

Nature is like a bank. It will return your deposit to you with interest. But if you don't make any deposits, you will get nothing. Here, the deposits are human values like love, selflessness, patience etc, and the interest payable to you is happiness and satisfaction. If you deposit nothing, you will never get these returns.

IDEAS

148. A youngster, looking for a job, visited a few grocery shops. But there was no vacancy.

After a few days, he heard that a grocer he had met earlier, had appointed a new boy. He rushed to meet the grocer and find out why he hadn't been chosen.

"That boy approached us, and gave us a new idea," the grocer said. "He said that he has a bicycle, and he was ready to work as a delivery boy. With the fierce competition in this area, it has worked wonders. That's why we took him."

On his way back, the disappointed boy thought to himself, *I also have a bicycle. What I didn't have, was an idea.*

Reflection

Without ideas, knowledge will seldom be put to any use.

IMITATION

149. A man had an expensive Chinese crockery dinner set. The centre bowl was particularly attractive. Once, while washing it, the bowl hit a hard surface and a long crack developed in the centre. So the man decided to get two similar bowls and placed the order with a master Chinese craftsman and also sent the cracked bowl to him as a sample. After two weeks he got two new bowls, exactly like the one he had sent as a specimen. The craftsman had taken extra pains to create the crack at the centre of the new bowls.

Reflection

If you blindly follow someone, no matter how great he is, you are likely to pick up some of their imperfections.

150. It was very dark along the village road and the car's headlight was not very powerful. So the man decided to follow the red tail lights of another car in front of him. Suddenly the other car stopped and he crashed into it.

This is my garage. go back to yours.

"Why didn't you signal that you were going to stop?" he complained.

"In my own garage?" asked the other motorist.

Reflection

Blindly following others can be harmful.

IMPRESSION

151. A youngster entered a crowded railway compartment and kept on disturbing the other passengers through the two-hour journey. While he was getting off at his station an old gent called him and said, "Young man, you left something behind."

"What's that? Let me take it," said the youngster.

"A very bad impression," replied the old gent.

Reflection

Many times people do things that only create a bad impression about themselves. But, unfortunately, they fail to realise this and do not change their behaviour, in fact they erroneously think that people appreciate the way they project themselves.

INFORMATION

152. A member of a hot air balloon expedition team was forced to land in the countryside due to a snag in the burner. He didn't know where he had landed. So he walked for three miles, till he finally spotted a small shop. He told the old man what had happened and asked him where he was.

"Right now you are standing in front of me in my office," replied the old man.

"So, you are the accountant of this firm!" asked the balloonist.

"Yes, but how do you know?" wondered the old man.

"Because your information is totally accurate, and absolutely useless," replied the entertainer.

Reflection

While accuracy is important, usefulness is also equally important.

INJUSTICE

153. Foreman: Didn't I tell you to see when the glue boiled over?

Workman: I did. It was at exactly quarter past eleven.

Reflection

Because most people do not respond to injustice, cruelty, and inhumanity, this world has become a bad place. One must never ignore injustice, one must raise one's voice against it.

INSULT

154. A salesman, who had worked in the field for 20 years, asked a newcomer, "How are you getting along?"

Would you like to buy Something? ? ?

"Very badly," replied the youngster. "I am insulted wherever I go."

"I don't understand," said the old timer. "I have been doing this work for 20 years. Several times I was manhandled, thrown out from houses, thrown into the gutter, held by the collar and tossed downstairs, but I have never been insulted."

R e f l e c t i o n

Depending on your ego, an 'insult' is either a fact, or just someone's personal opinion. A person with a huge ego feels insulted even by the slightest comment and therefore people tend to not express their opinions in front of them.

INTELLIGENCE

155. For an ordinary man before marriage, all girls are beautiful; after marriage, only the wife is beautiful; five years after marriage, it is only the wife who is not beautiful, all other girls are beautiful.

R e f l e c t i o n

For an intelligent man, beauty depends on one's perception. So, by adapting one's perception one can meet one's requirements and enjoy life.

156. There was a dog that would start barking through the night, without ceasing, whenever it saw the moon. But the moon never stopped shining.

Reflection

An intelligent man performs good deeds while giving criticism as much importance as the moon gives the barking dog.

---

157. Alcoholic: Water has killed more people than liquor.

Teetotaller: What do you mean by that?

Alcoholic: Every year floods kill thousands of human beings.

Reflection

A fool tries hard to justify his beliefs. A wise man believes in something, after it is justified.

---

158. A little boy said to his friend, "My mother gave birth to a baby. They didn't tell me whether it is a boy or a girl. So I don't know whether I am a brother, or sister."

Reflection

Most people lead a confused life. They do not have a pattern to follow in life. They will look at others to decide whether to smile, or curse. But an intelligent person behaves according to his/her own feelings, irrespective of the behaviour of other people.

159. Hungry, exhausted, and frightened, a hunter dropped his rifle, stumbled forward, and threw his arms around the man who had just emerged from behind a patch of timber.

"I am glad to see you," he cried. "I've been lost for two days."

"What are you so glad about?" mumbled the other hunter. "I've been lost for a week!"

Reflection

One will realise the value of fellow human beings only when one is in trouble. But, an intelligent man understands this even in good times.

INVENTION

160. "In our house, we have something that helps us see through the walls."

"Really! That is wonderful! What is it?"

"It is called a window."

Reflection

If used the right way, even the smallest and simplest invention can be wonderful.

JUDGING

161. A small boy came back home from the house of his new neighbours and said, "Mammy, you know, our new neighbours are very poor."

"How do you know that?" asked the mother.

"They were very worried when their little girl swallowed a 50 paise coin."

Reflection

Often we judge people's actions like small children do,

without finding out the real reason for their behaviour, although this leads to incorrect conclusions.

---

162.   After conquering a country, the king and his army were returning to their country. They had to pass through a desert where they ran out of water.

"What will you give a person who gives you a cup of water now?" the minister asked the thirsty and tired king.

"I can give him the country I just conquered." replied the king.

"So you have sacrificed so many lives and conquered a country which could have been won with a cup of water!" wondered the minister.

Reflection

Kind words and kind acts can win more than a battalion can.

KINDNESS

163. An optician was teaching his son the tricks of the trade.

"Son," said the optician, "once the customer likes the glasses he will ask you for the price. Tell him that it costs Rs. 100 and see his reaction. If he is not worried, add 'for the frame'. Then tell him that the glass will cost another 50. Again check his reaction. If he is still not looking worried, then add 'each'.

Reflection

The person who can judge people well, will be able to get a lot out of them.

KNOWLEDGE

164. The man who held a Masters' degree in Agriculture was critical of old-fashioned farming methods and told a villager, "You have to change your methods of cultivation. You see this tree? I would be surprised if it yields even 20 kg of apple in a year."

"I would also be surprised," replied the peasant. "It is a Chiku tree."

Reflection

For a happy and successful life, being down-to-earth and patient is more important than having degrees and leading a rich lifestyle.

---

165. *The one thing common among great people is their 'ignorance'. Socrates said, "I know that I know nothing," and he is considered to be one of the wisest men to have lived on this planet.*

Once a lady detected a small mistake in the explanation of a colloquial word in Dr. Johnson's dictionary and rushed it to him. She demanded the reason for the error.

"Ignorance, lady, pure ignorance," the great man replied.

Reflection

One's courage to accept one's ignorance is proof of one's knowledge.

---

166. A youngster approached a well known Kung Fu master since he wanted to learn the martial art. The youngster was very intelligent and picked it up very well. After one year, the master asked him how he felt.

"I feel that I can take on a thousand people together," replied the youngster.

"Your studies are not sufficient. You have to learn more," the master told him.

So, the youngster stayed with the master for six more months. During this period the master taught him different kinds of attacks. At the end of this period, he asked the youth the same question. This time the youngster replied that he was confident of taking on a hundred people at a time. Then the master told him that his studies were not complete and asked him to stay for some more time.

After six months would go by, the master would ask the student how confident he was, and each time the number of people he could take on kept reducing. Each time the master told him that his studies were not over yet, and he was forced to continue.

This continued until one day the youngster said that he was confident of defending himself if there was an attack from one opponent.

Then the master said, "Now you have learned everything I know. Till now, you did not know all the methods of attacking and that is why you felt that you could defend yourself against many people. If your opponent uses all the attacking methods you can effectively defend yourself against only one person."

Reflection

Knowledge is the basis of understanding. Boasting shows one's ignorance.

LEARNING

167. A father, whose daughter was married only a few months earlier, caught hold of the broker who had arranged the marriage.

"You said the boy was very good and that he doesn't even know to play cards. But, he lost all the money that I gave my daughter in the card room."

"He lost the money! That's what I had said, he doesn't know to play cards," the broker replied.

Reflection

One should learn an art before performing it.

---

168. A little boy was asked, "Do you go to school?" "No," he said. "I am sent."

Reflection

Learning can be made attractive and interesting. If parents and teachers understand this, then children will want to go to school.

---

169.   One day Edison, was being congratulated by some of his friends for being a great inventor.

"I am not a great inventor. But, I am like a good sponge. I absorb ideas from everyone and use them well. The basic idea behind most of my inventions are from other people who were not able to develop it themselves."

Reflection

For successful people, every incident, good or bad, is an opportunity to learn.

170.   "Give me six boxes of mothballs" the man told the shopkeeper.

"But it was only yesterday that you bought ten boxes!" the shopkeeper exclaimed.

"Yeah," replied the man. "I've thrown a thousand balls and haven't hit a moth yet!"

Reflection

Understand the product before trying out.

LIFE

171. One has to die first to go to heaven.

Reflection

Life is a mixture of sorrow and happiness. One cannot always expect only favourable circumstances. The best thing is to learn to love life, irrespective of whether good things happen, or not.

LISTENING

172. Teacher: Sam, make a sentence with the word 'I'.

Sam: I is —

Teacher: Sam, you should always use 'am' after 'I'.

Sam: Okay, then... I am the ninth letter in the alphabet.

I won't Listen To Them

Reflection

Always give people an opportunity to speak, and learn to listen.

173. "Have you been to any other doctor before you came to see me?" asked the medic.

"No, sir," replied the meek patient. "I went to a druggist!"

"That shows how much sense some people have!" growled the doctor. "And what sort of idiotic advice did he give you?"

"He told me to see you."

Reflection

Listen more, talk less.

LIVING IN THE PRESENT

174. "Tell me, do you like going to school?" a man asked young Johnny.

"I love going to school. But after getting there I don't like it," answered Johnny.

Reflection

Make your journey enjoyable, even if the destination is not attractive.

175. A life insurance agent was trying his best to sell a policy to a client who was adamant and wanted him to come back next year. As a last resort, while leaving the client's office, the agent hesitated at the door and asked, "Whom should I check up with sir, if you are not here next year?"

The man purchased the policy immediately.

Reflection

The past is gone. The future is unpredictable. What is for certain is only the present. Hence, never postpone anything.

---

176. A priest asked a man, "You look too worried. What is worrying you?"

"I am worried about my future," replied the man who was a samaritan.

"What makes you worry so much about your future?" asked the priest.

"My past," replied the man.

Reflection

Every day is one's future and past. Today was your future yesterday and it will become your past, tomorrow. Therefore, if you learn to live today properly, you need not worry about either the future, or the past.

LOOK

177. "I don't like the look of that fish," complained a customer.

"If you are interested in looks," replied the shopkeeper, "why don't you take the goldfish."

Always look for usefulness, rather than looks.

LOVE

178. "Do you keep pencils in your store?" asked a young boy to a shop-owner.

"No," replied the owner joyfully. "I sell them."

Every human being is like a store and love is a commodity that has to be sold. Your success in this world depends upon your ability to sell this to fellow human beings without keeping it to yourself.

---

179. "You shouldn't marry Ravi," protested the girl's mother. "He earns hardly 200 rupees a week."

"It's okay, Mama," pleaded the daughter. "When you are in deep love, weeks pass by too quickly to spend even 200 rupees."

Reflection

If one is able to love totally, money is not at all important for a happy life.

---

180. "No Rahul," Nikita said firmly, "I cannot marry you."

He thought for a while and said, "All right. Now, what about all those presents I gave you?"

"I will return them all," she said acidly.

"That's what you are saying," he said. "But what about all those chocolates I gave your younger brother, bangles, and hairbands I bought for your sister, and the shopping I did for your mother?"

Reflection

Human relationships and love should be above money. Whenever concern about material objects overwhelms the relationship then it is as good as broken.

181. "Can you give me," inquired a youngster, in a greeting card shop, "something really sentimental."

"You could take this," the shopkeeper said, taking out a card, "'To the only girl I ever loved'."

"Yah, this is good," said the youngster. "Give me two, oh no...four... five of these."

Reflection

In the arithmetic of love, one plus one equals everything, and two minus one equals nothing.

182. "As soon as I came to know," said a lawyer to his friend, "that it was a crooked case, I got out of it."

"How much?" asked the friend.

Reflection

There are two types of people in this world. Those who try to accumulate things, prestige, money, status, etc, irrespective of whether it is right or wrong. And then there are those who are prepared to lose all these things for the sake of love and humanity. In the long run, the second category of people earns respect and leads a pleasant life.

MARRIAGE

183.   Husband: I am not able to believe that today is our 25th wedding anniversary. How quickly time goes by.

Wife: That's true. I still remember our first meeting in the train.

Husband: Yah, I had set the alarm at 4 o'clock to catch the usual train. The alarm clock didn't work and I got up at 6 o'clock and took another train in which I met you. If I get the fellow who sold that alarm clock to me, I will tear him to pieces."

Reflection

Marriage should be the union of minds so that the association gives happiness and satisfaction to both. If this union doesn't happen, life would be boring and miserable. Therefore, the success of marriage lies in the efforts put in by both the partners to fulfil each other's dreams.

MATERIALISM

184. A man approached the owner of a house near a forest and asked, "Did you set a trap near your front gate?"

"Yes," replied the house-owner. "I kept it there to trap the wolf."

"Well. You've caught one of your relatives in it."

Reflection

Materialism is like a trap. You acquire things hoping to keep away your worries. But, it mostly traps your happiness and puts you in deeper trouble.

---

185. The municipal chairman distributed leaflets requesting people not to throw litter around. Next day, the cleaning staff had to clear more litter from the streets, most of it was the chairman's leaflets.

Reflection

Materialism brings a lot of litter in people's lives. Also, faulty religious practices adopted by them adds more to the clutter. If one wants to clean up, one should transform and lead a proper life instead of bending things to suit one's own convenience.

MATURITY

186. A man received a call from his friend at 2 am.

"What do you want?"

"Nothing specific."

"Then why did you call at this unearthly hour?"

"Because it is cheaper to call at this time."

Reflection

Maturity makes one realise not to pick up things just because it is cheap, or free. A mature person collects things only if they are required.

MEETING

187. A useless meeting is one in which minutes are kept despite wasting hours.

A useful meeting is one in which hours are utilised, irrespective of whether the minutes are kept or not.

MISERY

188. Reporters were interviewing a 100-year-old man.

"What is the secret of your long life?"

"Every day when I get up I have two options — to be happy, or unhappy. For 100 years I chose to be happy."

Reflection

Human misery is not by chance, but by choice. If one decides to be happy, there are plenty of ways of doing this.

MODERN TIMES

189. A young artist approached the organising committee of a grand art show. With great difficulty, he convinced the committee to display one of his pictures during the show.

He visited the exhibition to see his picture. To his shock

he found that his picture was hanging upside down. He rushed to the chairman of the committee to point out the mistake.

"But," replied the chairman, "the committee refused to accept it the other way."

R e f l e c t i o n

Today, as perception towards life has changed due to modern thinking and practices, a natural and normal life looks upside down to many people. But you are the artist of your life and you should perceive it properly, irrespective of how others see it.

MONEY

190. A girl had an affair with a rich man and became pregnant. On learning this, her father became furious and took his gun and reached the rich man's house. The rich man realised the danger and told the girl's father, "I know your daughter is carrying my child. But just listen to me for a moment before you do anything. If she delivers a boy, I have kept half a million dollars in the bank for him. If it is a girl I will increase it to one million dollars."

The father stood motionless for a few moments and

then said, "But sir, if something goes wrong, that is if a miscarriage were to happen, would you mind giving her another chance?"

Reflection

If one changes one's stand and loses one's integrity for money, then he/she will never be able to enjoy life.

---

191. "I heard that you are engaged to a girl staying close to your house."

"Yes, I am."

"But you told me that you are engaged to a girl residing in the next town."

"Yes, that is also true."

"How can one get engaged to two girls simultaneously?"

"It is possible. I have a car."

Reflection

Almost all problems arise from the belief that money will help one achieve anything (including the disrespect of people around you).

MOTIVATION

192. The boss made a surprise visit to the city office and found his manager kissing the pretty secretary.

"Do I pay you for this?" demanded the boss.

"No, you don't pay me for this. But I don't mind," replied the manager.

Reflection

The best way to motivate people is to make their work interesting.

---

193. During a press meeting, a journalist asked the chief executive of an organisation, "How many people work in your organisation?"

"Ah," the chief pondered, "I would say... about half of them."

Reflection

The success of an organisation lies in its capacity to motivate all of its employees to make their best contribution.

---

194. A supervisor made a surprise visit to a worksite and found a workman sleeping.

"Why aren't you working?" shouted the supervisor.

"Because I didn't know you were coming," came the reply.

Motivation is the best way to get work done, not via constant policing. A motivated worker will work hard even when he is not being supervised, whereas a 'policed' worker won't deliver even while he is being supervised.

---

195. The proprietor of a small business decided to improve the work flow in his office. So he bought a message board and fixed it on the wall. 'Do it NOW', he wrote on it.

His action had an immediate effect. But, not the one he wanted.

The cashier escaped with Rs. 30,000. The manager was missing, and so was the secretary. Workers gave a strike notice asking for a salary rise.

The best way to improve efficiency at work is to make employees responsible for their actions and to make the work interesting.

196. Once, three men working in the defence office of the erstwhile USSR were arrested and put in jail. One of them explained the reason for his conviction, "I came late for work. They accused me of being lazy, and thereby guilty of stopping the socialist progress."

"I came early," said the second man, "and they accused me of being a spy for the capitalists."

"In my case," told the third convict, "I came on time and they accused me of owning an American watch."

A manager's capability should be judged by his capacity to motivate his subordinates, not by his ability to accuse them. Unfortunately, several managers accuse, rather than motivate. Such managers are more 'damagers' than 'managers'.

197. A small king was attacked by his mighty neighbour. After the first day's battle, the king thought he would surely be defeated. He called all his men and said, "Yesterday night God appeared in my dream and said that we would win. To prove this I will toss a coin as he advised. We will win if it is heads."

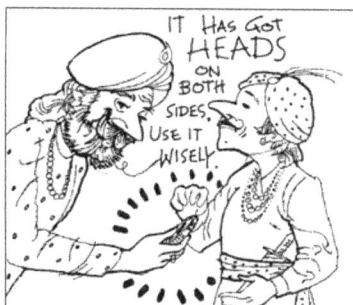

Then he tossed the coin and it turned out to be heads. All the soldiers felt hopeful. The king tossed the coin five more times, and each time it was heads. The soldiers were now really motivated and the next day they defeated the enemy.

After many years when the king's son was given the responsibility of the kingdom, he handed over the coin and said, "Son, this is a valuable coin. It has heads on both sides."

Reflection

A leader creates a team from a group of people, and motivates them to perform well beyond their capabilities.

NATURE

198. A tourist said to a hotel receptionist, "Are your rooms quiet?"

"Yes, of course," replied the receptionist, "It's the people who make the noise."

Reflection

Everything in this world is beautiful. It is us who make it ugly.

NOVELTY

199. A quarrel ensued between a multi-millionaire and a poor man about money.

"Do you know who I am? I have a 5000 sq. ft bungalow with a swimming pool and a theatre," declared the millionaire to impress the poor man.

"Many people have swimming pools and theatres," told the poor man.

"Inside the house?" questioned the millionaire.

"It is not a great thing," said the poor man. "I have got five sheep, ten chicken and ten ducks in the house."

"Many people have sheep, chicken and ducks," countered the millionaire.

"Inside the house?" asked the poor chap.

Reflection

One need not be wealthy to do novel things. Also, it is wrong to think that things done by spending plenty of money alone are novel. Many good things can be done without spending even a single paisa.

OBSERVATION

200. A scientist conducted a series of experiments on a frog. He kept the frog on a table, banged the table and said 'jump'. The frog jumped.

He removed one of the forelegs of the frog, banged the table and said 'jump', the frog jumped. He cut the frog's other foreleg and said 'jump', the frog jumped.

Then he repeated the experiment after removing a rear leg, the frog jumped again, but with great difficulty.

Finally, he removed the last leg, banged the table and shouted 'jump' the frog didn't jump.

He reached for his diary and wrote, "When all four legs are removed, the frog becomes deaf."

Reflection

If you make wrong observations, the decisions will also be wrong.

---

201. A research fellow was conducting a study on intoxication. He mixed some brandy and water and drank it, he felt intoxicated. He tried whisky and water and felt even more light-headed. To his astonishment he found that rum and water also had the same effect on him. He concluded that water is a strong intoxicating agent.

THE MOST
INTOXICATING
LIQUID
water

Reflection

The root cause of most wrong decisions is wrong observations.

OLD AGE

202. It is better to live as an 80-year-young person, than a 20-year-*old*.

Reflection

Most old age problems are not associated with the body, but with the mind.

ONE AT A TIME

203. "Are you married?" the census officer asked a villager.

"Yes," replied the villager

"Children?"

"Yes, five boys and four girls."

"That is… um… nine all together."

"No. One at a time."

Reflection

People who do one thing at a time achieve more than those who attempt many things together.

ORGANISATION

204. There is an organisation where the only human employee seems to be the Chairman. All other employees are cattle. Only during the Chairman's visit will the office be cleaned, on other days it looks like a cattle shed. On the day of the Chairman's visit, the snacks seem to be made for humans, on all other days it is similar to the food served to cattle. During the Chairman's visit, employees are served tea and snacks in clean crockery, on all other days it is served in dirty crockery.

Reflection

This is the case with most organisations. People present themselves like cattle by showing too much care during the visit of a top-notch executive and ignoring their own basic needs on other days.

---

205. A policeman on night duty was robbed by a gang. The inspector while taking down his report asked him whether he had his pistol at the time of the incident.

"Yes I had," the policeman

replied enthusiastically, "I kept it safely, so that they couldn't steal it."

Reflection

Organisations provide a chair for individuals to sit down, and power to take decisions, not for sitting around and admiring the quality of the furniture.

---

206. A person had the habit of sending letters and greeting cards to his friends and relatives at regular intervals. Every month he used to spend Rs. 150 200 on this exercise. Then suddenly the postal department doubled the tariff rates. It compelled him to cut down on the unnecessary mail.

Reflection

Every organisation incurs lots of unwanted expenditure which is cut down only when money issues crop up. Successful organisations foresee these problems and try to check wastage. There is always the possibility of saving on some resource.

---

207. A police officer (fed up with the amount of paper work he had to do) said, "I'm just a glorified stenographer in uniform. If I lost my pen it would be more serious than if I lost my gun."

R e f l e c t i o n

In many organisations, executives end up doing too much paperwork, and not anything intellectual. A manager should assess such situations and change them. With the enormous scope of IT and office automation it is possible to avoid too much paperwork.

---

208. A man from the south visited a city in the north. In the bus he asked for a ticket, 'to the central station'.

He was given two tickets. He thought that this was the system in the city. But later at the station he asked the conductor why this was done. The conductor had misunderstood what the man had told him, and thought 'to' meant 'two'. He refunded the money for one ticket.

Next day, while travelling to the station, the man told the conductor, '*for* central station'.

He was taken aback when he was given four tickets.

R e f l e c t i o n

Every organisation should study its systems and processes to check that it is convenient and easy to use by its clients. Any system, which is inconvenient, should be discontinued.

---

209. Two lawyers, after a tough verbal duel in court, were seen having lunch together. A person asked them how they could be so nice to each other after such a scene in court. One of them said, "We are successful in our lives and profession because we learned to have a difference of opinion and still be friends."

Reflection

Different ideas are required for the development of any organisation. Since different ideas come easily from different people, it is the basic requirement of the organisation to have a difference of opinion among people. But what should be learned and understood is that the professional difference of opinion should not reflect in personal relationships.

---

210. The boss asked an employee to get some urgent work done.

"I will get it done," he promised.

"No, you *do* it. I am *getting it done*," replied the boss.

Reflection

If everybody in the organisation is trying to get things done without anybody really doing it, it would be disastrous.

PARENTING

211. One four-year-old was telling his mother about his day at school.

"When Rama wanted Hanuman to go to Lanka," he said. "He went to the south and caught an Air Lanka flight from Chennai airport and flew down to meet Ravana."

"Is that the way your teacher told you the story?" the mother asked.

"Not exactly," he replied. "But if I told you the way the teacher told me, you would never believe it."

Reflection

The exposure children have to information makes them more mature than children from the previous generations have been. They are a mix of child and adult minds. So they require some logic and some wonders, unlike the earlier generation when children required only wonders.

---

212. He was brought up as a very disciplined and obedient child. Later, when he grew up, he was arrested and given a 10-year jail term just because he was obedient and disciplined… he was obedient to a notorious gangster and had become a disciplined smuggler.

Reflection

Children should be taught reasoning more than blind obedience, and discipline. Obedience prepares a child for becoming a slave to somebody else's ideas. Reasoning helps fit ideas into a frame according to one's own life.

---

213. A police officer said to the father of a boy caught stealing, "This is the third time he has been caught. Why don't you show him the right way?"

"I showed him the right way. But he keeps making mistakes and gets caught," replied the father.

Reflection

It is impossible to correct the younger generation if the older generation is leading an unclean life.

---

214. A small boy had the habit of sucking his thumb. His parents tried all sorts of things to rid him of this habit, but without any success. Finally, they stitched him a pair of loose trousers which the boy had to hold up with both his hands. Then he couldn't take off his hands for sucking his thumb and this cured him of his bad habit.

Reflection

There are several small tricks which can be used for correcting and guiding children. These methods could be more effective than threats and punishments.

215. Little David was the only son and his parents wanted to see him become a great man. So, they tried their best to teach him lots of things and make him 'number one' in school. But David could not grasp the subjects well and failed in the exams. His parents were exasperated and lost interest in life.

One day, after many years had gone by, David's parents had gone to town and noticed that a football match was going on. David's parents thought they would be cheered up by seeing the match.

Incidentally, David was playing for the local club. The opponents had a very strong team and the local club had little chance to win. But David played well and during the last few minutes he went charging towards the opponent's goal post. The crowd screamed, "David has the ball. He will score a goal. David is great."

David's parents who were enjoying the match, joined the crowd, "David will score a goal. David is great.... David is great...."

Reflection

Every child is special in some way. Sensible parents should identify what their child is good at and try to strengthen that skill, rather than trying to change the child to make him/her like something they do not like or have a talent for.

---

216. A naughty boy was caught sitting on a tree, plucking fruits.

"Come down this moment," shouted the furious owner of the farm. "Or I will tell your father."

"You can tell him right away," replied the boy. "He is sitting two branches above me."

Reflection

When it comes to children, evil is not generated, but planted in their minds by the behaviour of the adults around them.

---

217. A boy in the Fourth Grade was asked to spell 'raw'.

Upon spelling the word correctly, the teacher congratulated him and asked him if he knew the meaning of the word.

"Yes, of course," replied the boy. "It means without soda or water."

Reflection

Children learn from their elders. If their behaviour is inappropriate the elders should be held accountable.

---

218. In the 19th century, there was a priest in the United States, who firmly believed and preached, "It is wrong for man to fly. It is against nature. If God wanted us to fly, he would have given us wings! It is foolish to believe that man would be able to fly like birds."

This priest had two sons. The world knows them as the 'Wright Brothers', who flew the first aircraft.

Reflection

Throughout human history, children have been forced to think like their parents. Only a few children have managed to get out of this and think on their own. That's why there are not many people like the Wright Brothers, Galileo, Copernicus, Einstein etc. Good parents would help their child think on its own, instead of stuffing the child's mind with their own ideas.

---

219.   "Anu," asked mother, "if rice is selling at Rs. 12 a kg, how many kg will you get for Rs. 72."

"A little over 5 kg, mum," replied Anu.

"Why? Anu, that isn't right," said the mother.

"Yes, I know it isn't right," replied Anu. "But they do that."

Reflection

The best way to teach a child is to show them the right way.

220.   A middle-aged couple desperately wanted to learn Chinese. When they were asked why they wanted to learn the language with such urgency, the husband replied, "We have adopted a six-month-old Chinese baby. We should learn Chinese before it starts speaking. Or else, we may not understand what it says."

Reflection

A child learns from its parents. Whatever it becomes is because of the foundation laid by the parents.

221.   "My father fought in the India Pakistan war, my grandfather fought in World War II and my great-grandfather in World War I," boasted a fellow.

"Couldn't they get along with anybody?" asked another.

Be proud of being a peacemaker, not a warrior. One can destroy one's enemy by making him a friend.

PERFECTION

222.   A 20-year-old girl would respond to marriage proposals by asking "How is he?" She wanted to marry the nicest guy in the town.

At 25 her priorities changed, "What is he?" She was ready to make some compromises. He needn't be the nicest guy, but he should have a good job.

At 30 she was desperate and just asked, "Where is he?"

In life one should not wait for perfect things. Get what is available and work on it to make it perfect.

PERSEVERANCE

223. A villager got a bundle of Rs.100 notes. He started counting the notes. When he had counted 63, he stopped and kept the bundle in his pocket and said, "If it is right till 63, it's probably right all the way."

Reflection

Do not give up on anything while you are still half-way through.

---

224. A small boy was learning to ride a bicycle. After a short time, he fell down and got hurt. Still he was not willing to leave the bicycle.

"You are hurt. Why don't you leave it now?" asked a passerby.

"I got this cycle so I could learn how to ride, not to leave it," replied the determined boy.

Reflection

If people have the determination to fight till the end, there would be no work left unfinished.

POSSIBILITIES

225. There is a famous football puzzle — the football championship was just over. 24 teams had participated. Not a man scored a goal.

How could this have happened?

The answer is very simple. It was a women's championship.

Always think of other possibilities before reaching a conclusion.

---

226. Doctor: Now just step on the scales. There you see your weight! Now look at this chart. You're overweight.

Patient: No. I am not overweight. I am just five inches too short.

Every problem can be perceived in different ways.

PRAYER

227. A person went on a pilgrimage to a famous and crowded shrine. It changed his entire life. From that day onwards he succeeded in whatever he did. After some years while narrating the story of his success in life to his friends, he spoke about his pilgrimage. "The temple was crowded. When I reached close to the deity, the priest told me 'keep moving, keep moving'. I took this as advice from the deity and kept on moving and got here."

Reflection

It is not significant how many times one prays in a day. What is important is what one does.

---

228. Once a man was driving a cart that was loaded with goods. On the way, the cart's wheel got stuck in the mud. He started beating the bullocks to get them to move and pull the cart out, but the bullocks could not do this as the cart was heavily loaded. So he kneeled down and started praying to God. On seeing this, God got angry. He appeared in front of the man and said, "Hey, get up you lazy man. It is not my job to pull out your cart wheel from the slush. You get up and push. It will come out. You ask me for strength to do your work, don't ask me to do your work."

There is no sense in praying without first doing what can be done.

229.　A lone Chinese traveller was seriously injured in an accident and was taken to a missionary hospital. As his condition worsened, he was given oxygen and food through tubes.

As per the custom of the hospital, a priest used to visit all seriously ill patients and pray for them. When the priest concluded his prayer near the Chinese, with great difficulty the patient said, "*Minch chanki sai.*"

The priest didn't understand what the Chinese man said. So he bent down and repeated his prayer. The moment he stopped, the patient said again, "*Minch chanki sai.*"

A little bit confused, the priest again repeated the prayer a bit loudly. Throughout the prayer the patient tried to say something and finally uttered in a very feeble voice, "*Minch chanki sai,*" and died.

Later, out of curiosity, the priest who has memorised the words asked another fellow missionary, who knew

Chinese, what the meaning of 'minch chanki sai' was. The missionary said it meant, "You are standing on my oxygen tube."

Reflection

One cannot pray by just chanting, or singing songs. Prayer should be done by extending help to others, not only fellow human beings, but everything in nature.

PRESENT

230. A man presented his deaf girlfriend a parrot, which could sing like an angel.

"How is the bird?" he checked after a few days.

"It was very delicious," came the reply.

Reflection

While presenting something, the receiver's interest should be kept in mind. Otherwise, the gift will not have any value.

231. A beggar approached a hotel-owner and asked for help. The hotel-owner was not ready to give him

any money, but he offered him food. Unfortunately, it was late at night and nothing was left in the hotel except coffee. The beggar took three cups of coffee. Next morning as the hotel-owner came to open the restaurant, the beggar came there and punched him on the nose.

"What are you doing?" shouted the owner. "I gave you coffee yesterday. Is this how you show your gratitude?"

"You and your coffee! It kept me awake all night," the beggar shouted back.

Reflection

Help those who really need it.

PROBLEM SOLVING

232.   Here is one popular four-step problem-solving technique:

Step I: There is no problem

Step II: There is a problem, but it is not serious

Step III: There is a serious problem, but it will not affect us. Hence, we need not do anything about it.

Step IV: There is a serious problem. It will affect us, but it is too late to do anything about it

Reflection

Often, due to lack of proactive thinking, people fail to foresee problems. Due to lack of analysis they do not understand the seriousness of the problem, due to lack of concern they avoid action, and when it becomes serious they will not be able to do anything. Being proactive, having analytical skills, and concern for others will not come from outside. These are all in-built. One has to bring these out through continuous efforts and practice.

---

233.   The house was very close to a busy railway junction. The new tenant complained to the house-owner that the noise disturbed him. The house-owner pacified him and said he would get used to it in a month's time.

"Then I will occupy this house after one month," replied the tenant.

Reflection

One cannot solve a problem by keeping away from it. One has to face it.

---

234. It was his first journey on a ship. He was a little nervous when the ship started rocking due to strong winds. On seeing his nervousness an officer on the ship, consoled him and said, "Though we are in the middle of the Indian Ocean, land is only 3 km away."

"Only 3 km?"

"Yes sir, only 3 km, straight down."

Reflection

If one is ready to look around, there are solutions to any problem.

---

235. Johnny: Mommy, mommy, can one water a cow when it is thirsty?

Mum: Yes, you are right.

Johny: Then I am going to milk the cat.

Reflection

There is no universal solution for all problems. Every problem has to be analysed to find a solution.

PUNISHMENT

236.   A Grade Three teacher asked her students to narrate any act of kindness they had shown towards animals.

"Once," said one boy, "I kicked Ranji for kicking a cat."

Reflection

Punishment should not be a punishment for punishment.

QUALITY

237.   After ordering 15,000 dresses from a manufacturer, a buyer asked, "How long will it be before you deliver them?"

"Thirty days" said the manufacturer.

"Thirty days!" protested the buyer, "Why! The good Lord took only six days to create the entire world."

"That may be true," said the manufacturer, "but have you taken a good look at it lately?"

Reflection!

While striving for higher productivity and meeting targets one should not forget quality.

RELATIONSHIP

238.   Girl: Are you sure that mine are the only lips you ever kissed?

Boy: Yes, yes, and they are the sweetest of them all, also.

I wanted to prove that your LIPS are the SWEETEST in the world

Reflection

The most important thing in sustaining and enjoying any relationship is mutual trust and fidelity.

RELAXATION

239.   Once two reporters met Dr. Alexander Fleming, discoverer of penicillin, in a restaurant.

"Tell us Dr. Fleming," asked the reporters. "What is the great scientist in you thinking right now?"

"Very good question," replied the great scientist. "I was considering whether to have one fried egg, or two, for breakfast."

Reflection

However busy one is, one should be able to take his/her mind off work-related issues to relax. This will help immensely in personal and professional development.

240.   The King of Jha was a humorous man. Sitting on his throne, he used to crack jokes and also laugh heartily at jokes narrated by others.

But, his ministers didn't like this habit. One day they advised the King, "Our Lord! A King should be always serious and proud. Only then can he command his subject's respect. Otherwise subjects and enemies would take your Majesty lightly and it could lead to serious consequences."

The King smiled and said, "You have seen archers going to war. While going, they tighten the bow string because the tightness of the string decides the range of the arrow. After the war, they release the string, otherwise it will spoil the bow. The mind is also like this. At times when it is required one has to sharpen it and concentrate on serious tasks. Afterwards one has to relax. If the mind is always tense, it could lose its natural abilities."

Reflection

One should learn to take things seriously and at the same time relax one's mind. This will enhance one's capacity to do things.

RELIGIOUS PRACTICE

241. A farmer, lying on his death bed called his two sons and gave them his last piece of advice, "Do not sit down to eat, do not lie down to sleep, and do not go to the field after sunrise." And then he breathed his last.

Both the sons followed the father's advice. The younger one threw away all the chairs and cots and always stood up and ate and sat down to sleeping. He went to the field for only a few hours every day before sunrise and rested during the day. But, he became weak and his farm yield was low.

The elder brother was prospering. So the younger one asked him for his advice. On listening to his story the elder brother laughed and said, "You didn't understand father's advice and that's why you are in trouble now. By telling us not to sit down to eat he meant that you should eat only when you are hungry and take only what you want and not sit down just to finish the food you have. Father had advised us to go to bed only when we feel sleepy and not to lie down waiting for sleep. Thus, he wanted us to not waste time. By telling us not to go to the field after sunrise he meant that you should start work early in the morning even before the sun rises."

The younger man realised his mistakes and changed his daily schedule and became prosperous after some time.

Reflection

Most cultures and religions offer several good suggestions and sound advice about how to achieve success. Unfortunately, most of them are interpreted incorrectly. It is better not to practice religion or culture merely as rituals.

242. A blacksmith was instructing his assistant about how a horseshoe is prepared.

"I'll bring the horseshoe from the fire and keep it on the anvil. When I nod my head you hit it with the hammer."

The assistant did exactly as he was instructed. But the police arrested him for breaking the blacksmith's head.

Reflection

All cultures offer us good advice, unfortunately, we

misinterpret them, practice them incorrectly, and make our lives miserable.

243. A housewife tried to write down a recipe she was hearing on the radio. The reception was poor and she did not know that she was listening to two programmes from two different stations. Finally, she managed to note down the recipe as below:

"Take a cup of sliced onion, place it on your chest. Put a little salt in your nose. Now lie flat on floor and put a pinch of pepper into your eyes. Wait for ten minutes, your mixed vegetable soup is ready."

Reflection

The trouble with people is that they mix up the messages they receive from religion and the materialistic world and land up in a 'soup'. One should clearly define one's objectives and put in required efforts to achieve them.

244. A rich villager approached a doctor and complained of many ailments. The doctor couldn't diagnose anything particularly wrong with him other than a sedentary life.

"I think," said the doctor, "you lack exercise. From tomorrow onwards, you should walk ten kilometres everyday, and telephone me after six months."

After six months the doctor received a call from the villager.

"How are you feeling now?" inquired the doctor. "Hope all in your family are doing well."

"I am alright doctor," replied the villager. "But I don't know about my family."

"Why? What happened?" asked the doctor.

"As per your advice," said the man. "I started walking ten kilometres daily and in six months reached China. Now I am calling you from China to know what I have to do next."

Reflection

Every religion incorporates several instructions on how one can lead a happy life. But most people misinterpret these instructions. They get to some place other than where they ought to have reached if they had followed the instructions correctly. Therefore one should thoroughly understand the meaning and usefulness of rituals before practising them.

REPUTATION

245. A man who had the habit of carrying an umbrella with him wherever he went, found that all his

five umbrellas had some defect or the other. On the way to office, he gave all of them to an umbrella-mender and got into the local train. While getting down he absent-mindedly laid his hand on the umbrella of an old woman sitting next to him.

"Thief!" cried the old woman while snatching the umbrella from him, and the man felt ashamed and humiliated.

On his way back he picked up all the umbrellas from the mender. With five umbrellas tucked under his arm he was waiting at the bus stop when the old woman happened to come there. She stared at him for a while and said, "Had a good day, eh."

Reflection

Good or bad, one's reputation lives long in people's mind. Therefore always try to create a good reputation and live up to it.

---

246. A grocery shopowner was talking about his creditors.

"I never ask a gentleman for money."

"What you will do if he doesn't pay?"

"Then, after some time I conclude that he is not a gentleman and ask for my payment."

You, and only you, can make yourself lovable and respectable.

ROLE CLARITY

247. The trainer and the student were flying a small aircraft that was landing. The plane hit the runway and bounced many times before stopping.

"You made a poor landing," commented the trainer.

"Me," wondered the student, "I thought you were landing the plane."

Without clarity about roles, an organisation is likely to crash land.

RULES

248. "You should deposit your baggage in the cloak room before coming in," instructed the security guard in a famous museum, to a visitor.

"I do not have any baggage," replied the visitor.

"Then you cannot come inside. I have strict instructions not to allow anybody who does not deposit their baggage in the cloak room."

Reflection

Rules and regulations are made to make life comfortable. They should not be used to make life miserable.

---

249. Policeman: You can't park here.

Man: Why not?

Policeman: Read the sign board.

Man: I read it. It says 'Fine for Parking'. So I parked here.

Reflection

Understanding and defining rules correctly is essential.

---

250. A villager visited a prestigious museum. There he saw a signboard asking people not to spit on the floor. So he carefully spat on the roof.

MUSEUM ARTICLES

THOU SHALL NOT SPIT HERE NOR THERE

Reflection

If we interpret rules and regulations like this villager, we will transform this world into hell.

SELF-IMPROVEMENT

251. During his evening prayers, a school boy was overheard saying, "Oh God, please make Mumbai the capital of India." He kept on repeating this, and his mother became very curious.

"What on earth made you pray for that, my child?" she asked.

"I wrote that in my exam. I want it to be correct," the child replied.

Reflection

One should correct oneself, instead of trying to change others to suit one's convenience.

---

252. "There were two men senior to me," said the Professor addressing a crowd. "One was dismissed for being alcoholic, while alcohol led the other into crime,

and I am now head of the department. What has got me to this high position, I ask you?"

"Drink!" roared the enthusiastic audience.

Reflection

One should earn a high position based on one's merit, not on the demerits of others.

---

253. Husband: The food you make is not like how my mother used to make it.

Wife: That is probably because the money you make is not like what your father used to make.

Reflection

If we are as enthusiastic about improving ourselves as we are about asking other people to improve themselves, then we can achieve a lot.

---

254. One man was explaining to the other why he was getting drunk, "I got into wrong company. I had a full bottle of whisky and two teetotallers with me. So, I was forced to drink the whole bottle."

Reflection

The first step towards self-improvement is to learn not to blame others for your own mistakes.

---

255. A young man approached a famous sculptor and expressed his desire to become his student.

"I test people before admitting them as my pupils," replied the sculptor. "I will give you a test. You will have to make a statue using mud and it should have no defects at all."

The young man tried to do this, but failed. Every statue he made had at least a few defects. Frustrated, he told the sculptor, "I cannot make a statue without any defects."

"Then you can become my student," replied the sculptor. "One will learn only when one feels that they have not got knowledge on that subject."

Reflection

Those who feel that they know everything will never try to learn more and improve themselves. Understanding one's own ignorance is necessary before seeking improvement.

SELF-REALISATION

256.   A man wanted to sell off two acres of barren land, which he thought were good for nothing. He approached an agent. The very next day a newspaper ad appeared — *Two acres of land located near highway, with sufficient water suitable for agriculture, industry and residential purpose, for sale.*

After reading the ad, the man went to meet the agent and said "I have decided not to sell the land. After seeing your ad, I realised its potential.

Reflection

If you are not perceptive enough, you will curse your fate and it will take someone else to point out how lucky you actually are.

---

257.   Once a man approached a Zen master to achieve self-realisation. The master asked him to go out of the building and stand in the rain. After a few days, the man returned to the master and said, "I felt like a fool when I was standing alone in the rain."

"Very good. In the very first attempt you realised a lot about yourself," said the master.

Reflection

One who feels that he is 'big', never grows. One who realises that he is small will try and grow.

---

258. Teacher: Benny, your handwriting has improved a lot. I can read it clearly now.

Benny: Thank you teacher.

Teacher: But, now I see that you make plenty of spelling mistakes.

Reflection

Usually, most of our problems are hidden deep within us. We may not even know about it ourselves. For self-realisation one has to take stock of everything that we do and evaluate each action's merits and demerits. Then alone will we understand which mistakes we commit unknowingly.

---

259. Wife: Our maid took away two towels.

Husband: It is a pity. Some people are like that. Anyway, which ones did she take away?

Wife: Those that we had taken from the Palm Beach resort.

Reflection

It is easy to find faults with others without realising one's own faults. One who sees their own mistakes can succeed in life.

---

260.   A robber pointed a gun at an old man and shouted, "Give me all the money you have, otherwise I will knock your brains out."

"Okay, you do that!," said the old man. "I can live in this city without my brains, but not without money."

Reflection

If people have more faith in money than in themselves they are sure to invite trouble.

SICKNESS

261.   "How can one judge whether a doctor is an expert in his field, or not?" a junior doctor asked a specialist.

"Just observe the doctor," replied the senior man, "a good doctor, at least once in a while, will be able to tell his patients that there is nothing wrong with them."

Reflection

Sickness is caused by the malfunctioning of not just the body, but the mind as well. A good doctor will treat both together, rather than poisoning the whole body with only medicines.

---

262. A doctor sent a bill to a gentleman which read:

Fee for curing your father till his death: Rs.1,78,540/-

Reflection

Many people carry their problems with them until they die. One should always find out the reason for problems plaguing them and look for solutions.

SIN

263. A housewife told her friend, "The post office fellows are very careless."

"Why do you feel so?" asked the friend.

"Because," she said, "my husband sent me a letter from a town in Missouri and this post office clerk put the local seal on the envelope."

Reflection

Sins are like postal seals. However, hard you try to hide it, it will appear somewhere, getting you deeper into trouble. Therefore, desist from committing them.

SMALL BEGINNING

264. How many big men were born in Kolkata? None. Only babies were born in Kolkata!

Reflection

Everything is small at the start. Hence, take care of the small things so that they grow big one day.

SMARTNESS

265. A person living in the north, wanted to make quick money and therefore he printed about ten lakh Rs. 100 notes. After printing, he noticed an error. Though all the notes resembled the Rs. 100 bill, the figure on the note was '90' not '100'. He was upset as he

had invested all his savings on this project. He shared his problem with a friend who laughed and said, "That is no problem." He said there was a place in the south where he said all people were fools. He advised him to take the defective notes there and he would be able to exchange them for Rs. 100 notes.

Since nothing else could be done, he went to that town. When he reached there and walked out of the railway station he thought of testing the veracity of his friend's statement. He went to a shop and bought a pack of cigarettes for Rs. 10 and gave a fake Rs. 100 bill. The shopkeeper took the note, looked at it and put it in his till. The northerner was delighted. His friend was right. All fellows in this town were real fools. He would be able to exchange all his notes.

While taking the balance of Rs. 90 from the shopkeeper, he was taken aback to find, one was a Rs. 85 bill and the other a Rs. 5 bill.

Reflection

Do not underestimate others. Everyone has some talent.

266.   One day, while the country was under military rule, a peasant was arrested and locked up in jail. He received a letter from his wife who complained that she was having difficulties on the farm. She had plenty of seeds, she said, but she wasn't able to plough the field herself. He wrote back, "It's all for the best, my

dear. Leave the fields unploughed. That's where the guns are."

Four days later, two truckloads of special police went to the farm and dug it up.

Frantically, the wife wrote to her husband again to tell him what had happened and asked him what she should do.

He wrote back a brief note, "Now sow the seeds."

Reflection

If you are smart, getting things done is child's play.

267.   During his visit to New York, a British minister was determined not to play into the hands of the journalists.

"Are you planning to visit any night club during your stay in New York?" came the first query from a journalist.

"Are there any night clubs here?" the minister asked innocently.

The next day the minister was shocked to see the report of his

interview in the newspaper. The report said that the minister's first question on reaching New York was, "Are there any night clubs in New York?"

Reflection

One should always remember that there are other smart people around, so speak prudently.

SOCIALISING

268.   At the age of forty two, James was still a bachelor and didn't have any plans to marry.

"James," his father told him. "It is high time you got married. You see, at your age I'd been married for fifteen years."

"But Dad," protested James, "you married mum. I can't marry a stranger."

Reflection

Everybody is a stranger, until one starts socialising.

SUCCESS

269.   Most thieves are caught for something they haven't done... they haven't destroyed the evidence.

Reflection

In any profession, one has to pay attention to details to be successful.

---

270.   When the President visited an establishment managed by retired army veterans, all of them, wearing their medals with pride, came to receive him. Except for one veteran. The President shook hands with the old gentleman who wasn't wearing a medal and asked if he had not received a medal during his service.

"Yes I did," replied the old gent, "But I wear them only for special occasions."

Reflection

There are four types of people in this world. Those who know what to do, but do not know when to do it; those who know when to do something, but do not know what to do; those who neither know what to do, nor when to do it; and those successful people who know exactly what to do and when to do it.

---

271. Once, during the monsoon, a church was flooded. The priest climbed on to the roof and started praying. The water rose up to the roof. Luckily, a rescue boat came along and the boatman offered his help. But, the priest politely refused to get into the boat saying that the Lord would take care of him. After some time, the water rose up and it was up to the priest's knees. Another boat came by and the boatman offered to take the priest to safety, but he refused. The water then rose to his chest. A helicopter hovered over the church and the crew lowered a rope ladder. But, the priest refused and repeated that his Lord would take care of him. He eventually drowned.

In heaven face-to-face with God he fell to his knees and cried, "My Lord, I always believed in you. Why did you let me down?"

The God replied, "You fool, I never let you down. I sent you two boats and one helicopter. You refused them all."

Those who fail to grab opportunities, fail in life. Successful people are those who see an opportunity in everything and grab the first one.

272. A rich businessman was explaining the secret of his success. "Actually, there is no secret for success. One must jump at the first opportunity. That's all."

"But how will I know when the opportunity comes along?"

"That you cannot know," replied the successful businessman. "You keep jumping. It is very likely that at some point you will jump into the right opportunity also."

To succeed in anything, one must try, try, and try again.

273. Two salesmen were sent to two different parts of Africa by a shoe-manufacturing firm. The first man noticed that nobody in the area wore shoes. Disappointed, he sent a telegram to his manager, "Nobody wears shoes in this country. No scope for selling shoes."

The second salesman also noticed the same

phenomenon and sent a telegram to his manager informing, "Nobody wears shoes in this country. This is a tremendous market. Despatch the whole lot immediately."

Reflection

The difference between the successful and unsuccessful man is that the former sees a problem as an opportunity, whereas the latter sees it as a problem.

---

274.   An author met an editor and showed him an article, which had been rejected by the editor earlier.

"I had rejected this article last year. What is the idea of bringing this back to me again?" asked the editor.

The author replied, "You now have one more year's experience."

Reflection

People who see a problem in other people and want them to change without trying to change their own faults cannot succeed.

---

275.   "Can anybody spell 'camel'," the teacher asked in her class.

"Kemel," Jerry replied instantly.

After correcting him, the teacher asked, "How do you spell 'tiger'?"

"Diker," came the answer from Jerry again.

"Jerry, why don't you refer to a dictionary if you have any doubts?" asked the annoyed teacher.

Replied Jerry, "I don't have any doubt."

Reflection

Quite often people are very sure that what they are doing is right. Only after things go wrong, do they check their actions. But, if we have even a small doubt before starting something, we should be careful so that there are higher chances of success.

276.   Just when the football match was about to start, a sudden shower made all the seats in the stadium wet. People were hesitant to sit down till an enterprising newspaper boy said, 'Take a newspaper for one rupee and sit on it."

He converted a small calamity into a business opportunity.

Successful businessmen see an opportunity in a problem and those who find a problem in an opportunity seldom succeed.

---

277. Two strangers met in the vegetable market. Later that day they met again in a small factory.

"Oh, you work here!" said the first man. "I thought you were a farmer."

"I think," said the other man. "You made the same mistake I did."

A person who does not understand his own strengths and weaknesses and is unable to figure out where he fits in, will never be successful in life.

---

278. A boy in the sixth grade was punished for a prank. He had to run five times around the school. While running, the boy thought, "This is good exercise. I can do it everyday."

So he started running five times around the school everyday. The teacher, who had punished him, used to hang down his head and walk away whenever he saw the boy run.

Reflection

In life everybody comes across difficult situations. Only the person who understands this and converts problems into success can prosper in life.

---

279.   A political candidate went canvassing from home-to-home. He walked into a big compound and knocked on the door, a dog ran out barking. The candidate ran out of the compound. An old woman peeped out of the window and wanted to tell him that the dog wouldn't bite him, but instead, she shouted quickly, "What are you running for?"

"Municipal Councillor, seventh ward," he shouted back, without slowing down.

R e f l e c t i o n

To succeed, one should always have one's goal on one's mind, even during the most difficult situations.

SUSPICION

280. A politician decided to get married to a young woman. His experiences in dirty politics inspired him to appoint a detective agency to have a report about his to-be bride's private life. A month later, the agency submitted their report as follows:

"The young woman in question has very good character. All through school, till date, she has been well-behaved and is respected by all. All her friends belong to the elegant high class. However, of late, she seems to be slipping. In the past few months she was seen frequently in the company of a politician with suspicious character."

R e f l e c t i o n

If you are suspicious about everyone else, be careful, you might be in the wrong yourself.

TEAM WORK

281.   Police officer: You committed this theft alone?
Culprit: Yes Sir. You can't trust anyone in my profession.

Reflection

In any field, mutual trust and team work are important.

---

282.   Three leading surgeons were asked to perform a major brain surgery. After the operation, the surgeons were able to make the brain functional, but the patient died. When asked for an explanation they replied, "We are brain specialists. Our responsibility is to make the brain alright. In this case, the failure was in the heart. You speak to the heart specialist. As far as we are concerned the operation was successful."

Reflection

Without team work, any organisation will suffer such a fate. Individuals/departments will succeed, but the organisation will fail.

---

283.   After his death, a man was shown hell and the heaven. In hell he saw that everyone was being served hot soup and they had to drink this using a spoon with a 6-ft long handle. Unable to drink the soup with such a long spoon, almost all the people there were starving and were very weak.

Next, he was taken to heaven. The situation was the same. Everybody had a 6-ft long spoon to drink the soup with. But here, in spite of this, everyone was happy and healthy. He asked the angel how this was possible.

"In hell and heaven, the situation is the same. There is no difference except that in heaven people feed each other, and in hell they try to feed only themselves," said the angel.

Reflection

In today's world, only those who believe in team work can be happy and successful.

---

284.   A person asked a boy who caught a fish using bait, "You caught this big fish all by yourself?"

"No, I had a small worm to help me."

Reflection

Nobody can exist in isolation. Everybody is dependent on someone. One cannot achieve anything without the other's help. We should realise this and create an atmosphere conducive for coexistence.

---

285. A farmowner engaged four men to undertake cultivation. The first man was assigned the preparation of the land. The second man was asked to put seeds into the channels made. The third man's job was to cover the channels and the fourth man was in charge of watering the land.

As planned, the first man prepared the land. On the second day, the second man didn't turn up and hence the seeds were not sowed. On the third day, the third man meticulously covered all the channels and then the fourth man started watering the land. He did this for a long time, but no saplings were seen.

Reflection

Without team work, organisations seldom achieve results. There cannot be a totally independent job in an organisation. Everybody is inter-dependent. Hence each person in the organisation should help others and together achieve the organisation's goals.

---

286. Tom, Dick, and Harry were given a big data entry assignment by their boss. Tom and Dick worked

hard and finished most of the work. Then came Harry's turn, he finished entering the last few items and reported to the boss, "Those guys worked for more than 15 days without any results, but I worked for less than an hour and completed the entries."

Reflection

Most of the success achieved in an organisation is due to team work.

USEFULNESS

287. A guest asked a farmer, "What's that new building there?"

"Well," replied the farmer, "if I can find a tenant, it's a bungalow. If I can't, it's a godown!"

Reflection

One should be able to find a use for everything.

288. In a pet store: "I like this dog. But its legs are too short," said one customer.

"Oh, no madam," replied the shopkeeper. "All four legs are touching the ground."

Reflection

The most important aspect of anything is its usefulness. But any thing is worthless if it doesn't serve any purpose, however elegant it may seem.

---

289. A fishing net is nothing but a lot of holes tied together.

Reflection

Everything in the world, if utilised properly, is useful.

VISUAL MEDIA

290. The effect of television advertisements can be understood from the following prayer made by a small child, "Oh Lord, give us oven fresh, vitamin enriched, protein packed, delicious, nourishing, wholemeal bread."

Reflection

Visual media is highly effective in influencing people. It has its uses, but it can also be misused.

WISDOM

291. Two colleagues were talking about their office.

"The boss mildly suggested some changes," said the first man, "and his suggestions are always implemented."

"It always happens that way," replied the second man. "The boss's mild suggestions get priority over the heated arguments made by others."

Reflection

One should try to acquire so much knowledge and wisdom that even one's suggestion is respected by others.

WOMAN'S LIFE

292. Woman: What do you think about women trying to imitate men?

Man: They look like fools.

Woman: Then they are successful in their efforts.

There are plenty of enjoyable things in a woman's life.

WORK

293. The punishment for ordinary crimes is a jail term and a lot of work. The punishment for serious crimes is solitary confinement without any work.

Sitting idle is much more difficult than doing hard work. So, learn to enjoy work.

---

294. I had a dream. I died and reached a lonely place. The whole day I rested. Then I felt bored. I shouted, 'Is there anybody here?' Immediately a man appeared and asked what I wanted. 'What can I get?' I asked. "You can get whatever you want," the man said.

So I told him what I wanted and in no time he brought all that I had demanded. I ate well, drank, and rested for a few more days. Whenever I wanted something I called out and the man gave it to me. After a few days, I was bored with the idleness. Then I asked him to give me something to do.

"But that is the only thing I cannot give you. I cannot give you any work," he said.

"Ah, I feel miserable," I said. "I would rather go to hell."

"Where do you think you are now?" asked the man.

Reflection

A life without any work and human relationships is miserable. One should realise this and enjoy one's work, and one's fellow human beings.

---

295.   "Take a week's notice. You're sacked."

"But I haven't done anything."

"That's why you are sacked."

Reflection

One can tolerate a person making mistakes, not one who is idle.

---

296.   A mother to her daughter: Anu, haven't you got your shoes on yet?

"Yes, mom. All, except one."

Reflection

Often, people take up very small assignments, ask for a long timeframe and still don't complete the task. Then come the justifications — 'I have done everything except a few', etc. These few things may make up more than 70-80% of the total assignment.

---

297.   A firm contacted a new employee's previous employer to ask for a reference. Soon came the reply, "He is highly responsible. Whatever went wrong in our organisation, he was responsible."

Reflection

One should try to be an asset to the organisation one is working for, and not a burden.

---

298.   The secretary, excusing himself for being late, said that his watch was too slow. The boss replied, "You must get a new watch, or I must get a new secretary."

Reflection

This statement should be remembered by every one in their day-to-day life.

---

299.   In a progressive organisation, people are hired, not for doing things, but for improving things.

Reflection

Remember, if you are not improving things, you are not earning your salary.

MISCELLANEOUS

300. A ripe mango fell from a tree. An ant came that way, saw the mango and realised it was very heavy. So, it called its friends to help take it away.

Next day another mango fell. This time a goat saw the mango. It ate the mango in ten minutes.

The third day, a cow saw the mango. It ate the mango in a gulp.

Reflection

When one talks about the size of a problem, he is actually referring to his own size. If someone says 'I am too busy,' he means that he is too small for the job he is doing. If you are big, the problem becomes small, and vice versa.

---

301. "I am scared," a man told his friend. "I got a letter from a guy saying that he would kill me if I don't keep away from his wife."

"Well, keep away from his wife," his friend advised.

"But I don't know who he

?!!

But He Has Not Written His Name

is. He has not written his name," he said.

If you keep making mistakes, you may escape a few times, but not always.

---

302.   A young composer once came to Mozart for advice on how to develop creativity. "Begin writing simple things first," Mozart told him, "songs for example."

"But you composed symphonies when you were only a child," the man exclaimed.

"Ah," Mozart answered, "but I didn't go to anybody to find out how to become a composer."

Learn from others if you want to know only the basics. Learn from your common sense if you want to become a master.

---

303.   After performing magic tricks in a street corner, the magician passed around his hat. It came back empty. He looked at the hat, smiled and said, "Good! I got my hat back."

Reflection

One should be able to find something positive in even the most disappointing situations.

---

304.   Once, while travelling by train, Albert Einstein bought a newspaper from a vendor. But he soon realised that he had left his glasses at home. He therefore requested the vendor to read out the headlines for him.

"I'm also illiterate like you, Sir," came the reply.

Reflection

People see themselves in others. One has to be good to see what is good in others. If you only see the other person's faults then there is something wrong with you.

---

305.   His parents always told him that only God knows everything. He believed that and never tried to equate himself with God. So he always said 'God only knows.' He died without doing anything and without knowing anything.

R e f l e c t i o n

If one starts doing things, one will know many things which 'God only knows'.

---

306. A successful organisation is a group of ordinary people doing extraordinary work.

307. A doctor said to the patient, "Exercise kills germs."

"But Doctor, how do I make these germs exercise?" a patient asked innocently.

R e f l e c t i o n

One should be able to look at the bigger picture.

---

308. Teacher: Tell me how fast light travels.

Student: The same way slow light travels.

R e f l e c t i o n

One should not just interpret things to suit one's own convenience.

---

309. "Please close the window. It is cold outside."

"If I close the window, will it be warm outside?"

Reflection

People want warmth, not from within, but from outside. We want everybody to change but we won't change ourselves. As long as this attitude prevails, people will not improve.

---

310. A young mountaineer looked nervously at the steep cliff that his guide was proposing he should climb.

"Do people often fall off the top?" the trainee asked.

"No," said the guide. "Once is usually enough."

Reflection

We live only once and every moment happens only once. Hence, one should utilise one's time extremely carefully. One wasted moment is a wasted moment for ever.

---

311. The fire station received a phone call, the caller sounded frantic, "Hurry, my house is on fire. Please come fast."

"How do we get your house?" asked the fireman.

"Why!" wondered the man on the other end of the phone, "don't you still have that big red truck?"

Reflection

One should be able to look at all the alternatives before reaching a conclusion.

---

312. "Where does Dracula stay whenever he visits the earth?" a minister asked during the prayer meeting.

"After seeing the way my office is kept, I believe, Dracula prefers my office," came the reply.

Reflection

Offices are meant for human beings, not for Dracula. Housekeeping is very important to keep people comfortable and drive Dracula away.

---

313. "Does your watch tell the correct time?"

"No, my watch does not tell me anything. You have to look at it to know the time."

Reflection

Even the smallest activity in the world requires effort. Whatever one gets without making an effort will be worthless.

---

314. "We had our Granny for last new year eve," a small boy told his friend.

"Really?" wondered the friend. "We could manage only chicken."

Reflection

Correct perception is required for visualising things correctly.

---

315. A couple didn't want to be recognised as newly-married. So they wore old-fashioned clothes and pretended to ask the hotel receptionist casually, "We would like to get a double bed with a room, please."

Reflection

Never allow eagerness and anxiety to take control of you.

---

316. Which is the longest word in the English language?

SMILES — There is a mile between the first and the last letter.

When you use the longest word, you will get the largest benefit. Hence, always remember to put this word into action.

---

317. Two hundred people were travelling in a train compartment during a hot summer day. While the train stopped at a station, a passenger saw that the next compartment was empty. He looked into the crowded compartment and announced, "The next compartment is empty. Why should we sit in this crowded compartment?"

So all 200 got off and entered the next compartment.

Blindly following others will almost always lead you into trouble. Follow your own consciousness, it will lead you to prosperity.

318. A diamond becomes shiny and attractive only after a very hard polish.

Reflection

One can bring out the best in people by putting them into difficult situations only to make them realise their potential and ensure their development, not for taking revenge.

---

319. "You were proposing marriage to a silly girl some time back. It would be better to get out of it."

"I am already out of it."

"How did you get out?"

"I married that girl."

Reflection

Often, the best way of avoiding a dilemma is to do something about it.

---

320. An umbrella-mender was given an umbrella to repair in a countryside home. He was very careful while repairing the umbrella. The owner of the house noticed this and said, "You are very careful while repairing the umbrella. You may probably not come this

way again to get more business. Then why are you taking so much care?"

"You are right sir," replied the umbrella-mender. "I may not come this way again, but some other person will. If I do a good job you will not turn your face against him."

In every walk of life, there are people who take extra care while doing their job even when it does not give them any benefit. In organisations, such people should be identified and rewarded. In the long run, any organisation will benefit because of such people.

---

321. In Hyderabad a man wanted to see the Charminar.

He asked a man, "Does this road lead to Charminar?"

"Hao," was the answer.

He continued walking on the road. After some time he again asked a passerby, "Does this road lead to Charminar?"

"Hao," he got the same answer.

After some time when he didn't see Charminar, he asked a Nawab Saheb, "Nawab Saheb, does this road lead to Charminar?"

"Ji ham, Hujur," Nawab Saheb replied.

"Everyone said, 'Hao', but Nawab Saheb, you say 'Ji ham, Hujur', what is the meaning of all this?"

"They are illiterate. Educated people do not say 'Hao'."

"This means you are educated."

"Hao," replied Nawab Saheb.

Reflection

Practice what you preach, not just once or twice, but always.

---

322. An investment agent approached a businessman with new proposals.

"I'm quite busy today. Please tell me quickly what you have," said the businessman.

"The investment plans I have brought will earn you millions of rupees," claimed the agent.

"It's okay. Please leave your proposals with me. I'll have a look at it later. Now I'm working on a plan by which I am sure of earning Rs 653 in cash," said the businessman.

Reflection

One bird in the hand is better than two in the bush. Never

leave sure things for something which is not sure, no matter how big it is.

---

323. John saw a big man beating up a small fellow along a country road.

"Don't beat him," John shouted and knocked the big man down.

"Thanks," said the meek fellow. Then he opened a purse he was holding, took out Rs. 100 and gave it to John.

"It's your share of the money I took from him."

Reflection

Do not act without understanding the situation.

---

324. "Is that a popular song she is singing?" asked a lady at a concert.

"It was, before she started singing it," said the woman beside her.

Reflection

You will be accepted and respected only if your contribution adds value. Therefore while selecting your job, ensure that you are able to add value to it.

---

325.   One of the twin brothers became a preacher and the other a doctor. One day a gentleman met the doctor on the road and said, "I heard you preach yesterday and it was very good."

"I'm not the one who preaches, but the one who practices," replied the doctor.

Reflection

If only one could start practising all that one preaches, one would achieve all those things one wants to achieve.

---

326.   A man entered a doctor's office. "Doctor," he said, "Please help me. I had swallowed a gold coin about a year ago."

"Good heavens!" screamed the doctor. "Why have you waited for one year? Why didn't you go to a doctor immediately?"

"To tell you the truth," replied the man. "I didn't need the money then."

Don't wait for things to get out of hand.

---

327.   It is alright if one
drinks like a fish. The problem
starts when one doesn't drink
what a fish drinks.

One cannot succeed by doing the right thing in a wrong way,
or a wrong thing in the right way.

---

328.   A missionary was deep inside a jungle, and
came across a witchcraft practitioner who was beating
the drums furiously. "What is the
message you want to convey?"
asked the missionary.

"We have no water," replied the
witch.

"So you are praying for rain?"
asked the missionary.

"No," snapped the witch. "I'm sending a message to the plumber."

Reflection

Being remote from the centre of modernity doesn't mean being undeveloped (both physically or mentally).

---

329. This is a popular medical college riddle:

A doctor fell in love with a nurse and they got married. After one year they were blessed with a smart child. But the doctor was not its father and the nurse was not its mother. How is it possible?"

You are papa, not mummy. There is my mummy.

The answer is very simple. The doctor was a lady and the nurse was male.

Reflection

Never get carried away by paradigms. Always think about other possibilities.

---

www.ingramcontent.com/pod-product-compliance
Lightning Source LLC
Chambersburg PA
CBHW071430090426
42737CB00011B/1619